ISBN 978-1-331-28135-1
PIBN 10168490

This book is a reproduction of an important historical work. Forgotten Books uses
state-of-the-art technology to digitally reconstruct the work, preserving the original format
whilst repairing imperfections present in the aged copy. In rare cases, an imperfection in
the original, such as a blemish or missing page, may be replicated in our edition. We do,
however, repair the vast majority of imperfections successfully; any imperfections that
remain are intentionally left to preserve the state of such historical works.

1 MONTH OF
FREE
READING

at

www.ForgottenBooks.com

By purchasing this book you are
eligible for one month membership to
ForgottenBooks.com, giving you
unlimited access to our entire
collection of over 700,000 titles via
our web site and mobile apps.

To claim your free month visit:

www.forgottenbooks.com/free168490

English
Français
Deutsche
Italiano
Español
Português

www.forgottenbooks.com

Mythology Photography **Fiction** Fishing Christianity **Art** Cooking Essays Buddhism Freemasonry Medicine **Biology** Music **Ancient Egypt** Evolution Carpentry Physics Dance Geology **Mathematics** Fitness Shakespeare **Folklore** Yoga Marketing **Confidence** Immortality Biographies Poetry **Psychology** Witchcraft Electronics Chemistry History **Law** Accounting **Philosophy** Anthropology Alchemy Drama Quantum Mechanics Atheism Sexual Health **Ancient History** **Entrepreneurship** Languages Sport Paleontology Needlework Islam **Metaphysics** Investment Archaeology Parenting Statistics Criminology **Motivational**

THE JOURNAL OF

SIR ROGER WILBRAHAM

Solicitor-General in Ireland and Master of Requests

FOR THE YEARS 1593–1616

TOGETHER WITH NOTES IN ANOTHER HAND

FOR THE YEARS 1642-1649

VOL. X.　　(w)

THE

JOURNAL OF SIR ROGER WILBRAHAM

[Wilbraham was over in England in the spring of 1593, in attendance on the Privy Council (' Cal. of State Papers, Irish Series,' 1592–6, pp. 77, 89). In September 1593 he was back again in Dublin, as is shown by his writing to Burghley there-from (*ibid.* 144).]

10 *Aprilis* 1593 : At th'ending of parliament,[1] Cook [2] sollicitor, speeker ; Puckering [3] l. chauncelor ; before the coming of the Queen, two of the privi councell delivered the act of general pardon to the l. chauncelor. After the Specker & Commons brought in : & then her maiestie came in her robes & coronett, & having well placed & settled her self, the Speeker & 2 or 3 & most at barre after 3 low congeas, made an oration : 1° of the antiquitie of parliament used in king Ebe's [4] tyme : secondlie of her maiestie's favor in calling her people to consult for the state : & 3° desired leave to compare her maiestie to a bee : which governs with such pollicie that all thother obey : *et rex sine aculeis*—the master bee without stinge : and so her mercy such as never punisheth without remorse : then her people are valient as bees to drive away the drones : so they put Spaniards to flight : & said the bees brought honey to Plato an infant : which fortold his eloquence & wished the same hap had befallne himself to utter his ; 4° he shewed the nobles & commons had made lawes to which her maiestie must give lief or els they now determined : viz : lawes & statuts con-tinned : other lawes capable of lief if her maiestie by her voice

[1] The dissolution of this Parliament is described by Heywood Townshend (*Historical Collections*, pp. 45–49, ed. 1680) and D'Ewes (*Journal of Parliaments of Elizabeth*, ed. 1682, pp. 465–467). There are considerable vaiiations in details from the account here given, but the substance is similar.

[2] Sir Edward Coke, the future Chief Justice of the King's Bench, at this time Solicitor-General and Speaker.

[3] Sir John Puckering, Lord Keeper, 1592–6.

[4] Ina (D'Ewes's Report, p. 465).

gave them lief as laws newlie established: first for repressing
inward disturbers as papists & scismatikes: secondlie a provision
against invasion: offering in the name of all a treble subsedie &
6 fiftenths acording to ther habilities not answarable to ther
myndes, who were willing to loose ther hartes in the enimies
bosome for her safetie: 5° rendred her maiestie humble thanks
for her gracious & ample pardon: & because it extended to facts
done before the parliament, therfor craved a special pardon for
his defects or offences done of ignorance & so ended.

The l. keper having kneeled before her maiestie retorned to
his place & said, ' Mr. speker her maiestie hath hard your eloquent
& wise spech & geven me expresse commaundment to answare to
some partes thereof: & 1° to the antiquitie of parliament an
allowed thing: & King Canute used it: 3° aproved the comparizon
of the bees, & extolled her clemencie & allowed the subiects' valure
& dutie, onlie charged some of oversight that in the lower house
gave not due reverence to some of her privi councell: 4° the lawes
she allowed: and persuaded the iudges & magistrates to see them
executed—*magistratus est lex loquens*: acepting most thankfullie
the subsedie, as a provision against invasion: and persuaded that
the musters & armer might be well regarded: '

Then her maiestie stood up saying to this effect: in golden
wordes. She thought meete the Lords & Commons should understand out of her owne hart & mouth those thinges the l. keper
had spoken by her direction: 1° touching the subsedie she
thanked them assuring them that it was for their own defence a
provision & not for her expenses: for her endevors were spent
altogether either in service of god: or in government of her
people or for the florishing estate of her kingdomes: her care
was as great as any kings had been (her father excepted in
reverence of a child) to preserve her people: that she was now
groen in yeres & therfore not like now to bestow her treasure but
for the safetie of her people: that since the beggininge she bathe
refused good occasion to amplifie her kingdom: but that she
feared it wold be more charge to her people then honor: she
never gave occasion of offence, wherfore her neighbors should so
anoy her: she made warre abroade to kepe it farther of: she
required none to feare: her hart never stood so much at peace ·
she knew no cause to doubt victorie but persuaded provident provision & so ended with hartie thaunkes.

29 *April* 1593 : before her maiestie at Whitehall : the recorder of London [1] & aldermen presented the L. maior [2] : the recorder's speech was that the armor of peace was the due administracion of the sword & of lawes : for as treasure is called the sinewes of peace : so the administracion of lawes are : in both which he extolled her maiestie's most happy government as well with her power against foes as Justice towards her subiects : then he discended to shew that king John, 16 of his raign, incorporated London & endowed them with manifold liberties, that the maior chosen should be presented to the l. keper : then to the barons of eschequer or lieutenant of the tower : after to her maiestie : by whose graciouse raigne and benignitie the citie had florished above all the rest of the realme : wherefore in humble acknowledgement thereof ther service goods & lives were redie to sacrifice to her gracious pleasure : prainge that her maiestie wold vouchsafe to geve allowance to ther choice, for that the l. keper & lieutenant had allowed him : being chosen acording to ther charter's limitations : beseching pardon if in this or his last spech he had committed any error :

The l. keper after her maiestie by whispering had intimated her pleasure said, ' Mr Wm Roe the Q^s most excellent maiestie hath hard and effectuallie perceaved your spech and geven me in charge (albeit an unworthie interpreter of so divine an oracle) to lett you understand her gracious pleasure touching some parts thereof : 1° touching your discourse of lawes she aproveth them true, requiring at your handes due administracion, within your liberties : for that in the rest of the realme the same is committed to careful and sufficient men : 2° wher you advaunce your citie before others, *tanquam inter viburna cupressi*, her maiestie taketh not your charters to bind her prerogative, but that by abuses the same are to be resumed : but if you speak it to record the great benifites you have receaved, then know your service and diligent preservacion of her maiestie's people & lawes are the more exacted at your hands : 3° your choice of a maior being acording to usage her maiestie graciouslie alloweth : & commendeth your wisdom to elect such a man : & her maiestie requireth you my L. maior (for so I may call you being so allowed by her maiestie) to have a

---

[1] Edward Drew, Serjeant-at-law and M.P. for the City 1593, was Recorder 1592-4.

[2] Sir William Rowe, Lord Mayor, 1592-3.

more special regard then usuallie hath ben, to attach and reforme seminaries & Jesuits, & the new Sectaries that refuse to come to churche: which lurke in London as the endlesse laberinth of England, for largenes & blind corners: also to have care to vagabonds & loose men that may upon occasion raise seditions and kindle a rebellious faction within your owne walles: to see wepons be not comitted to prentizes & servants, who some of them of late practized disorderlie attempts, but for preservacion of peace to comit wepons to the best citizen howseholders: to have better regard to avoid infecion that ther doors infected may be shut & marked: to avoid inmates acording to th statut: & so he was knighted:

The chief baron Manwood's[1] answare to a noble man's letter ·

> Malam causam habentes
> fugiunt ad potentes:
> Ubi deest veritas,
> ibi queritur potestas ·
> Sed vivat Rex
> et currat lex:
> And so I leave your Lordship:

Praunces Flowre[2] did were an H: sett with small rubies & diamondes, & under was written *dulcis asperatio hic haec hoc* · the allusion to the privilidg of printing grammer wherin *hic haec hoc* is the first lesson: also he said *hic* signified Sir Christopher[3] that obtayned his license: *haec* the queene that gave it & *hoc* the thing it self:

---

[1] Sir Roger Manwood, J. C. P. 1572; removed to the chief seat in the Exchequer 1578, occupying it for about fourteen years. (Foss's *Judges of England*, vol. v. p. 516). In Manningham's *Diary* (Camden Soc. vol. xcix. p. 91) the lines are differently given and the incident giving rise to them seems also to differ.

[2] Francis Flower an infringement of his Patent is recorded in *Acts of the Privy Council*, (N.S.) vol xiii. p. 88: June 19, 1581, and in *State Papers, Dom.* 1591_4, p. 11, February 19, 1591, there is a letter from him, dated at Sir Christopher Hatton's house in Ely Place.

[3] Sir Christopher Hatton.

Also in a harvest songe to entertayne her maiestie at Draiton ·
one singular verse was:

> Of Brittanie land
> she is the first, for hie desertes,
> that weres a crown of all mens harts.
> O gay garland : harvest home, harvest home:

Fletwood[1] old recorder asked what became of all his presse of
clients that wonted to follow sayd, 'god hath blessed me with long
lief, for all my clients be dead:'
Competencie with contentment is the fairest mark to wise desires : per Wilbraham

Manie knightes made nowadaies that have nether esquires'
living nor gentlemen's deserts:

Sir John Rainsforth[2] examined before Bonner touching the real
presence, said he beleved Jhesus Christ to be in the Sacrament in
the same maner & substance as he rid to Bethelem : namelie
in his botes spurres & cloke riding upon an asse : Gardener ·[3]

My L. Chaunccellor tels that capten Cuff writt of a lawier ·

> ' Iste fuit bonus vir propter scribere lex ·
> subter Henricus octo et Edwardus sex.'

Tom Luttrell served a privie seale in Graies Inne upon userer
Stukeley : he was espelled the house : for Anger & Whiskins con-
ceived all rich clients wold banish Graies Inne.[4]

---

[1] William Fleetwood, Recorder of London 1571-91.

[2] Sir John Rainsforth. In *Acts of the Privy Council* (N S.) vol. v. p. 328,
August 11, 1556, there is mention of a recognisance for 1,000 marks that he should
remain at his lodgings in London or within two miles of the same, and be forth-
coming when called for.

[3] Probably Sir Robert Gardiner, Ch. J. Q. B. of Ireland 1585-1604, with whom
Wilbraham was associated in several commissions in Ireland at this time. (*Acts
of the Privy Council* (N.S.) vol. xxiv. 1593, pp. 287 and 290.)

[4] Thomas Luttrell, Richard Anger or Aungier, and William Whiskins were all
members of Gray's Inn. Anger and Whiskins were old benchers and had held
the office of treasurer, while the date of Luttrell's admission is 1580. (*The
Pension Book of Gray's Inn* ; and *Gray's Inn Register*, J. Foster.)

Hibernia, 31 *Sept.* 1593. This day before the barons of eschequer the maior of Dublin[1] newlie elected was presented by the recorder with an oration that H 2 gave their liberties by name of a portryve : H 3 augmented them to a maire & sherives & to have the same liberties that the citie of Bristol had : & ther maire to be sworne before the chief governour : & because of his absence King E 3 granted power to take ther oath in absence of the deputie before the barons of eschequer at Dublin : & if theschequer were not ther, then the new maire to be presented & sworne before the old : & shewed ther elecion of Mr. Ryans maior : & in the entrance into his speches, how the people by nature rude & disorderlie were taught obedience by lawes : & lawes deade without magistrates, wherupon the first charter of H 2 was granted to Dublin :

Sir Robert Napper chief baron answared that he liked well the thankful remembrance to the Queene and her progenitors, & that the prince's favors had ben great & the citizens' desertes worthi all commendacions : he compared this politike bodie to a natural bodie . by a large resemblance : that the maior was the head & hart that guided & governed all the bodie : the hart was the lief of all the rest : for if that were not sound it yelded contagious blond to infect the bodie : but being pure, it being the vital spirite, to all the rest gave good norishment : the armes were the shiriefs : the sides the aldermen : legges the commonaltie : and said the maior was like the anker that held the ship : he persuaded the maior verie amplie to attend divine service & have all his bodie with him : that the cause whie people of late came not to church was for that Pius Quintus the pope, 20[2] of the Qs raigne, by his bull excommunicated the Queen : & discharged the people of ther obedience : which bull was after revived by pope Gregorie the 13 : doctor Saunders[3] & Allene[4] were the pope's nuntios in

[1] In the *Calendar of Ancient Records of Dublin*, vol. ii. p. 265, the name of the mayor at this time is given as James Janes.

[2] This should be 12 Eliz., *i.e.* 1570.

[3] Nicholas Saunders, the famous author of *De Visibili Monarchia Ecclesiæ*, who, landing in Ireland in 1579, incited Desmond to revolt, and perished there in 1581.

[4] Cardinal Allen, founder of the English College at Douay, who in 1588 published his violent pamphlet against the Queen entitled 'An Admonition to the People of England,' advocating the Spanish invasion of England and declaring the Papal sentence of excommunication against Elizabeth.

Ireland: what calamity ensued Irishe cronicles declared: he compared the Jesuits to vultures who as Plinie writeth were so suttel of smell, that the smell blond three daies before the bataille & would be 3 daies before at the place of bataille: he also compared them to the Harpies in Virgil, that were paynted like Virgins but devourers of men: & so Jesuites under simplicitie bring men to perdition: he said the sword borne before the maior signified justice & fortitude: the white rod temperance and innocency: & amplified that: & exhorted them to looke to the streetes & markets.

29 *Sept.* 1596: the recorder presented Chamberlain [1] maior before the barons of eschequer, saing in effect the came to deliver the sword & receve it ther as from the Quene.

He said manie held opinion that it was fatal to cities to have a certen begyning & a certen end, as the nativities of men were certen: told of divers histories that varie in the begyning of Dublin citie: & for the end it was as incerten: for Rome was conquered, Athens and Carthage distroied: & recited manie other cities and countreyes:

He showed this citie before the conquest, how it came by the conquest; that king H 2 conqueror first endowed them with Bristow liberties: and shewed that ech king hath enlarged somewhat: in specialti, and declared ther services in specialtie.

And with some examples out of Plutarche's Lives, he compared ther services: and commended them to be *illesœ fidei*; *virgo intacta*: & shewed ther choice & praied allowance of ther mayor:

Baron Segreve answared in praise of justice, exhorted him to government, and praised ther choice, and *juratur*.

Per W. Gerrard: [2] one said by Puckering L. keper: he was acquainted with him verie familiarlie, & had neither great lerning nor welth till that advauncement, but now he perceved the operation of a L. keper's place was to purchase a manor every moneth:

---

[1] Michael Chamberlain, Mayor of Dublin 1596_7 (*Cal. of Ancient Records of Dublin*, vol. ii. p. 298.

[2] William Gerrard, admitted Gray's Inn 1572: in the *Pension Book of Gray's Inn*, p. 99, there is an entry dated May 9, 1593, mentioning him as Clerk of the Duchy.

Tom Lancaster [1] said, Yelverton [2] was seriante, merite by course
of common lawe : Haries [3] et Glanvile [4] by Borow Englishe pre-
venting ther seignors : [5] but the rest by the statute of *Quia
emptores terrarum* :

[Wilbraham came over to England early in 1598 (*Cal. of State Papers,
Ireland*, 1598_99, p. 29), and, it would seem, settled down to practise at the English
Bar. (See Introduction.)

6 Daies past, viz. 9 *Feb* : the parliament of 39 & 40 R[ae] ended ·
her maiestie came to the house of the Lords and commons : [6] the
speker (Yelverton serieant) made a most fine & well filed speche :
verie short & manie well couched sentences somewhat imitating
but bettering Euphues : his exordium was, if any common welth
most sacred and renowned quene be to be acounted happie who
have free libertie to treate & enact lawes, & so wise & prudent
a prince to see them executed with justice & mercy, then is
England thrice happie : he exampled England with the lawes of
Solon, Licurgus & Plato : reciting some sentences of ech of
them : then he discoursed largelie how the commons had seriouslie
considered acording to the uttermost of their reaches of good
peticions as lawes for the kingdome : commending ther sinceritie
and gravitie : & that as new diseases require new medicins, so ech

[1] Thomas Lancaster, admitted Gray's Inn 1569.   Other jests of his are recorded
by Wilbraham.

[2] Christopher Yelverton, admitted Gray's Inn 1552, Serjeant 1589, Speaker 1597,
and J. K. B. 1602 (Foss's *Judges*).

[3] Thomas Harris, of the Middle Temple, Serjeant 1589.

[4] John Glanville, admitted Lincoln's Inn 1567, Serjeant 1589, J. C. P. 1598.

[5] Yelverton was considerably senior to Harris and Glanville, and evidently their
superior in reputation, having been Reader in his Inn in 1574, while Harris was
not elected a Reader till 1588 and Glanville only in 1589.   The other Serjeants
of 1589 were Edward Drew, John Cooper (Inner Temple), Thomas Hamond
(Gray's Inn), and Thomas Owen (Lincoln's Inn).   *Dugdale Chronica Series* (1680),
p. 99.

[6] Townshend does little more than give a bare record of the Queen's coming
and the two speeches here given. (Townshend, *Hist. Col.* ed. 1680, p. 126.)
D'Ewes (*Journal of Parliaments of Elizabeth*, pp. 546-7) has a somewhat fuller
account, but both in substance and in detail, so far as the speeches, at any rate
are concerned, is inferior to the report which Wilbraham has given.   In the Lord
Keeper's speech for instance the complaint concerning the Judges and Justices of
the Peace is omitted.

common welthe wilbe ruined unlesse ther be prevencion of daungerous enormities by the helpe of good lawes : which in course of tyme are to be abrogated altered and renewed as occasion is : & amplified this with some few sentences of histories : & said such yet was the condicion of these peticions wherupon the commons had assembled, consulted & resolved, that lik as the picture of Pigmalion with the painter himself for the rareness of the work was but a dead image until it pleased Jupiter to instill lief, so these peticions shalbe fruitelesse, unlesse it please your royall maiestie to inspire lief unto them.

Then he further presented in all humilitie a small subsidie, as an assured token of ther bodies lands & liefs to be entierlie devoted to princelie pleasure of so sacred & sovereign quene :

Hereupon he entered into discourse of her maiestie's manifold vertues : science of languages : especial favour towards her subiects, to dispend for ther defence her private treasure, which he acompted as peculiar to her private as the possessions of subiects : that her maiestie in regard to kepe her treasure for defence, had not bestowed it on private : that her maiestie did not delite in sumpteouse buildings, too great a fault in manie subiects : saying builders wold undoe themselves if enimies did not restraine them from ther owne destruction : 2° that she had ben princelie temperate in apparell : adding some sentence in the praise of moderation therein. So 3° likewise in banquetting praised her temperance with a sentence or twoe : he also spak of the execution of lawes : and Licurgus the best lawe giver, because his lawes were executed : Then he proceded to compare lawe for government & armie against force : & amplified that both were the parties of a prince : & that subsidies were to be geven for defence of kingedome : & provision made for withstanding raging enemies : by sentences : & her maiestie had a greater potentate her enemye then any her progenitors : namely Spaine, who sought the effusion of all English bloud : the exaltation of superstition &c. & invasion.

Then he in the name of the howse rendred thanks for that her maiestie had reformed noisome licenses, & privilidges called monopolies : he praised her maiesties justice, but especiallie her mercy which had eternized manie, with severitie seldom any : he craved pardon if the howse had transgressed ther dutie : and sithence none could speke for himself but he, craved upon his knees pardon for himself : this spech was full of elegancies, swetlie delivered: but thought too full of flatterie to curious & tedious :

Sir Thomas Egerton L keper : said her maiestie had given him expresse charge to answare to the learned & eloquent oration, commending his treatie of lawes : reproving the negligence in justices of peace & of assise in not providing for the pore : not punishing forstallers, regrators, ingrossing : not executing the statute of Winchester : that sturdie vagabonds & such pretended gents as wanted living, which as it was death in som common welths, so he wished it to be punished in ours : that justices of peace were lik dogges in the Capitoll, that being sett to barke at rebels, sett themselves to anoy the good subiects : so ther gredines was the grevance of the people :

That tho her maiestie provided this subsidie for safetie of her people she yet acepted it thankfullie & graciouslie as a gift to her self : amplified the rancorous malice of Spain : that all provision & redines was for withstanding him :

Amplified that of his knowledge living and dying he must acknowledge her maiestie never desired the wealth of her people nor annoyance, with hard extremities or without aparent right : he complayned that witt of man ill employed had invented enormous & pestilent perpetuities : which might have been converted to better purposes to the service of god & contrey : advised the Justices of lawe in her maiestie's name to make pleine & sincere expositions of the lawe, not to plauge themselves with curious interpretations, wherby any enormities might arize :

He cited some sentences of Jerome &c. of the blessings of a iust prince : prayed for her sentenciouslie & brieflie, & craved pardon for himself :

The acts read: and thassent royal notified : the L. keper declared her maiestie's pleasure to dissolve the Parliament.

Within 3 daies after the day after terme [1] the L. keper in full assemblie said he was commanded by her maiestie to deliver such things as herself if tym had permitted meant to have uttered in parliament : that all should repaire to ther howses & not dwell like battelors in London : that the should kepe hospitalitie for releaf of pore : that the lawes he spok of in Parliament & now againe renewed might be executed : that manie Justices of peace were baskett

---

[1] Hilary term ended February 21 ; the date would therefore be February 25, 1598.

Justices, to gather hens & capons *colore officii*, but not to distribute justice to the releaf of the subiects : that Justices of assize should not look to the clositt of rich princes &c. but the peace of the countrie : & as bishops had triennial visitations, so she sent them as visitors twise a yere : if they neglected the publick service she wold correct them, & they should be acompted as collectors not correctors : that principallie her maiestie's pleasure was ech should gard his owne quarter : look to musters and armor for provision : not upon any event shune from his howse for fear, for then her maiestie would sese his livings & correct him for cowardize by her royal prerogative : & as preparation was wisdom, so her hart feared nothing, but assured of victorie by gods hand. Under whose protection she erected safetie by her polesies : *posui Deum adjutorem meum ; scutum fidei protegit me* : & so with an eloquent & pithie speche ended :

The l. Treasurer commended the Justice of England now above former tymes : advised to Justices : complayed of numbers of Just[ices] of peace : & that lettres of musters should issue : that recusants increasing be looked to : &c.

Hughie Beston [1] works better with a rake then a shovel : per Hikes Avarus :

Tanfield [2] told Attorney Cooke, he was the best cook and liked his fingers best of any cook the Queen had.

Aprill 1598 : Maries rehersal sermon : [3] *flores* :

[1] Sir Hugh Beeston, of Beeston, Knight, son of Sir George Beeston, who died in 1601, aged 102. Sir Hugh died in 1626, aged 56. (Ormerod's *Hist. of Cheshire*, 2nd ed. vol ii. p. 272.)

[2] Lawrence Tanfield, admitted Inner Temple 1569 : J. K. B. 1606 and C. B. Exch. 1607 (Foss's *Judges*).

[3] On Good Friday a sermon was preached at *Paul's Cross* on Christ's Passion : and on Monday, Tuesday, and Wednesday in Easter week sermons were preached at the *Spital* or pulpit cross of St. Mary's, Spitalfields, ' to persuade the article of Christ's Resurrection.' And then on Low Sunday a learned divine at *Paul's Cross* made ' *Rehearsal* of these four former sermons, either commending or reproving them as to him by judgment of the learned divines was thought convenient. And that done, he was to make a sermon of his own study.' The Mayor and Aldermen attended these sermons. (Stowe's *Survey of London*, edited by W. J. Thoms, and note thereto, p. 63.) See also *Remembrancia, City of*

Alexander when he built a citie made 4 gates to receve in the 4 windes to purefie the citie : so this citie had 4 sermons to purge it from synne : & so compared ech sermon to some of the windes : with sentences in praise of some of the windes : & acording in ech place praised their severall sermons : no knowledge, but Christ and him crucified, with all the sermons preached.

3 captens praised in the new testament : S Mathew : of one Christ said he had found no such faith   27 Mathew : another capten confessed god.

Cornelius a capten in the acts of apostels : a devout man : an almes gever : &c.

So also the poet says, *nulla fides pietasque viris qui castra sequuntur.*

Yet the scripture aproveth the profession of armes lawfull by these good men.

Another saeth, *exeat aula qui vult esse pius* :

Ambrose saiethe, *non agnovit elemosinarium pervenisse ad malum finem.*

Salomon praied that God wold nether geve him nether povertie nor riches, but convenient to live on :

1°. Samuell : vers 16 : [1] God tooke away his good spirit from Saule & the evill spirite tormented him ; which proveth a good & evill spirit :

Englands blisse by the long and prosperous raigne of her Maiestie during whose government 5 popes, 2 French kinges, have died : [2] many other neighbouring kings princes & dukes poisoned and murdered.

Vertue geves the most resplendent lustre :

Graunt's [3] sermon upon Cornelius, Acts, &c., & whose notes for the most part the forsaid were, wished with Cicero : that it was

---

London, 1579-1664, pp. 367-8, where the City asserts, to the Council, its right of appointment of the preachers at *St. Mary's Spital* on the three usual days in Easter week : ' though they had usually acquainted the Lord Bishop of London with their names that he, knowing who they were, might the more fitley appoint a preacher for the *Rehersal Sermon* at *Paul's Cross.*'

[1] 1 Sam. xvi. 14.

[2] As a matter of fact there were eight popes and four French kings between 1558 and 1598.

[3] Dr. Edward Grant, Camden's predecessor at Westminster School, a scholar poet, and preacher.

written in every mans forhead, *quid de religione et republica sentiret*, at this day so many camelions and doble faced Janus be [in] ech place :

23 *Aprilis* 1598 : was I at St Georges feast : kept at Whitehall : the Earle of Shrewsberie was L. President of the order : for that day : L. Admirall[1] eldest : erle marshall[2] second : Lord Buck hurst 3 : Erle North[3] 4 : L. Tho Howarde 5 : Erle Worcester 6 : L. Hundesdon 7 : L. Mountioy 8 : Sir H. Leye[4] 9 :

On the eve about 3 of the clocke were all the servants about London that attended on the knights of the order of the garter in the baze court, inner court hall and elsewhere : but now admitted into the presence : then the knights as they were attyred in their robes : being purple velvett all & trayling on the ground : lyned with white taffita, for lightnes as semed : the inner garments were ther ordinarie hose and doublett : with a side casesocke beneth the calf of the legg of scarlett coloured velvett : & a hood of the same like a livery hood but larger torned on the right shoulder : & on ther left armes the read cross embroidered on ther utter robe · ech had a velvett cappe and fether : saving the L. Buckhurst : who belike doth not professe armes but a councellor : he had no fether : the bishop of Winchester[5] was prelate of the order, onlie in a purple velvett robe : the deane of Windsor[6] in succession is deane of the order : & had a crymson satten robe : one of the gent ushers, Mr. Conesby[7] is gentleman usher of the black rodde : (with which he useth to goe before noblemen & peers that are attainted. or to suffer :) ther were two harolds kinges & about 12 more other harolds in ther richest attire : that went in procession & to chappel before ther lords

After eche was thus richelye attyred : the Lords passed throw

---

[1] Charles, Lord Howard of Effingham, at this time Earl of Nottingham.

[2] Robert Devereux, Earl of Essex.

[3] Roger, Lord North, was not a Knight of the Garter : and his name is erased in the MS.   [4] Sir Henry Lee.

[5] Thomas Bilson.   [6] Robert Bennett.

[7] On November 14, 1601, complaint was made in the House of Lords on behalf of Mr. Connisby, Gentleman Usher, that in the last Parliament the Serjeant-at-Arms had been employed in bringing in persons before the Lords upon breach of privilege of the House, whereas this duty belonged to the office of the Gentleman Usher. (Townshend, *Hist. Col.* ed. 1680, p. 133.)

the presence to the Q^s Maiestie, soveraigne of the order : to waite
on her to chappell : her maiestie went not : so the went after the
harolds to chappell : the youngest knights formost : two and two
in a ranke : & the President last alone : every two together made
in the chappell two solemn curscies, one I thinke to her maiesties
place, thother to the presidente : before the took ther seats,
ordinary praiers : one chapter read by the Prelate of the order
thother by the deane : the rest of praiers said by the L. Prelate : 2
psalmes and two antems songe with great melodie, organs, voices,
shakbuts and other instruments : & so after 2 solemne curseis departed the chappell and retorned in order to the Presence : & ther
attending for supper : the L. President sate on the left hand close
to the clothe of estate : & the whole table about 40 dishes, the first
course sett dishe upon dishe : all doble gilt plate was for the
L. President's messe :
. 2 tables more, whereto were 3 messe more, sate all the rest of
the Lords and knights of the order : ech one a yard and a half
from another : all upon the benche : served in silver with meate
as much as could be couched on the bord : as tho ech had a messe
by himself : to ech messe two courses & a bankett : the meate was
brought up by the gards : but the ordinarie Queen's shewers did
not waite : but to ech knight one of the gent Pensioners & another
gentleman appointed to attende :

Before & after supper, standing water was brought, first to
the president with 3 congees : whom ech knight attend bare :
after to ech two knights water brought againe by other, & so in
order ech washed with the hatts on : with like three congees two
chaplens said grace : & so sate at supper : wherein they spent
2 howres & a half : & at tenne of the clock departed to ech ones
lodginge :

During this tyme of supper all the tables in the Q^s howse
supped in ther due order, & I supped at the L. chamberlayne's [1]
bord : where Sir John Poines [2] was his deputi :

[1] George Carey, second Lord Hunsdon.
[2] Probably Sir John Poyntz, of Iron Acton, Gloucestershire. Aubrey, in a
note on his son, Sir Robert Poyntz, speaks of the family as having been 'men of
note at Court' (*Brief Lives*, A. Clark, vol. ii. p. 172). He does not seem to have
actually ever held the post of Vice-Chamberlain, which would appear to have
remained vacant between the death of Sir Thomas Heneage, in October 1595, and
the appointment of Sir John Stanhope in 1601 (*S. P. Dom.* 1598 and 1601, pp.

The next day her maiestie went to chappell in procession under a canopie caried with 6 : & that knights all :
Die sequenti, Comes Essex cum 300 : et Baron Mountioy cum 200 servis marched to the L. maior.

Ultimo Aprilis 1598 : Crook [1] Recorder: grant maior de Londres fuit fait chivaler : fait oration a cet efect
Exordium : the earth most dred & gracious soveraigne brings forth no such weede so hatefull as an unthankfull man : the subiects of England never more bound to so gracious a soveraigne who by her magnanimitie hath preserved us from all daungers feared as invasion : &c. : & by her prudence unspotted iustice provident & unspekeable bountie hath conferred upon her people all graces as peace, plentie, iustice tempered with mercy : &c. upon these he amplified but not longe : then he proceded to praise her maiestie's magnanimitie, & all the 4 cardinall vertues by name, & her sinceritie in true religion more worth then all the blessings that any kingdome might expect : namelie all honorable vertues in the nobilitie ; sanctimonie in the clergie : integritie in iudges & magistrates : probitie in the people : he touched *obiter* as a praise, that her cities were inriched & garnished with the spoiles of her proudest enimies (meaning Spaine) ; then he shewed brieflie that the citie according to the customes had chosen M[r] Saltingstow L. maior, humblie praying her gracious aprobation to give lief to ther election ; & as in all thankfulnes they acknowledg her innumerable princelie bounties, so are they in all unfainednes redie with all ther lands goods & lives to do all humble services.
Sir Thomas Egerton L. keper, answered that by her Maiestie's direction her Maiestie apointed him to declare that she acepted those praises not as merited by her ; but as remembrances what vertues were to be embraced by one in her high place : yet she acepted it as an increse of God's mercy, that those blessings had happened to her people under her government being the weker sex : that she desired no longer to live then might be for the

103, 227). In *S. P. Dom.*, 1598-1601, p. 544, Feb. 3, 1601, Sir John Stanhope, before his actual appointment, is mentioned as appointed to serve as Vice-Chamberlain in the absence of the Lord Chamberlain.
[1] John Crooke or Croke, of the Inner Temple, Recorder of London 1595-1603, and Speaker of the House of Commons in 1601 : J. K. B. 1607 (Foss's *Judges*).

welfare of the people: remembered them of ther great bounties & privilidges: required carefull government of the people, in peace.

Cooke attorney, at dinner, Whitsonday: 98: ista protulit: Wolsey a prelate was *flagranti crimine* taken in fornication by Sir Antony Pagett [1] of the West, & put in the stokes: after being made cardinall, Sir Antony sett up his armes on the Middle Temple gate: the cardinall passing *in pontificalibus*: & spying his owne armes, asked who sett them up: answare was made the said M[r] Pagett: he smiled saying, he is now well reclaymed: (for wher before he sate him in disgrace, now he honored him.)

27 Numeri [2] voet que daughters inheritera: et terre ne doet linealment ascend: et par ceo il confound un civilian devant le sieur Tresorer:

Esdras [3]: est dit que 6 partes de terre est pour planting et sowing et le 7 part pur mare: ergo il collect entant cosmographers font le mere tant que terre, que tout le terre nest trove:

Il montre auxi a nous un late liver de discoveri de un Hollander ove wonder:

Il dit que Judges adiudg que clerke de markett quant il ad pritt fee pur ensealing measures, ne poet apres aver fee pur vewing de eux, coment il ad ete issint use par prescripcion, mes doet present le offenders et certifie ceo:

He said he had seene an old statute not printed of 46 E. 3 wherein it was enacted, no noble nor other should have any more but two dishes at the first course & two at the second: & porage acompted for none ·

Nil facit reum nisi mens rea: Sieur Keeper Egerton, *Camera Stellata*.

Phisicioners say corrupcion of blond & inflamation of blond be severall infirmities, but both mortall to the bodie: so is wilfull or rashe periurie mortall to the state: & therefore, to be punished sharpelie: Essex, *Camera Stellata*:

Seriant Yelverton said a pore bachelor to be maried had no money to pay the prist, only 8[d]: the prist in congregation refused to mary him without full pay: he desired he might be maried as

---

[1] Sir Amias Paulet in Cavendish's *Wolsey* (ed. Singer, vol i. p. 6).

[2] Num3ers xxvii. 8: 'If a man die, and have no son, then ye shall cause his inheritance to pass unto his daughter.'

[3] 2 Esdras vi. 42.

farre as his money wold go & promised to pay the rest: & so was: the priest after asking the dett: nay said he, I will geve 10 tymes as much to unmarie us:

Sir Rendall Brereton [1] told that one asked the Vicar of Acton [2] when he wold bestow a wief, on him that he might geve him thanks: " since I live by the fruites of my benefice: & have maried 1000 coples in this parishe: not one that ever came to geve me thanks."

My L. keper at dinner said it semed a hard praier: "God save, defend me from the fair grace of God: " viz. when one hath broken his arme with a fall, that he brake not his neck is called in Cheshire the faire grace of God: & "god defend me from the Q^s gracious pardon," meaning that he never stande in daunger of hanginge or neede of pardon.

For 3 causes it is better in warre to be assailant then defendant: first the assailant is commonly more coragious: 2° the sodennes of encounter doth often astonish the defendant: 3° chieflie to make warres by assailing need but one part strengthened: but defensive warres must fortifie manie tounes for defence: not knowing wher the enemi will assaile or make discent, and so hath need of more men.

Ariosto desired the rather to die because the lernedst divines say we shall know one another after this lief:

The precher at Powles told of a man that rode on an ass & left his yonge sonne page like foote: the passagers called him unnatural: he made his sonne to ride behind him: then were they called eruele to overloade the asse: then both went on foote & led the asse: then both were acompted sottishe: at last they carried the asse that should have carried them: & so were counted worse then asses to carie an asse: at laste they resolved to do what best liked them: for every action is scandalized by *Momus* or *Zoilus*.

Doctor Kayus,[3] he said he wold not in his will nominate either

---

[1] Sir Randle Brereton, second son of John Brereton of Eccleston and Wettenhall (Ormerod's *Cheshire*, vol. ii. p. 195), admitted Gray's Inn 1553 (*Gray's Inn Admission Register*, 23).

[2] Acton near Nantwich. John Lowe was vicar 1559–1601. The manor was bought by Roger Wilbraham in 1602, and passed over to his younger brother, Ralph. (Ormerod's *Cheshire*, vol. iii. p. 345.)

[3] Dr. John Caius, the founder and first Master of Gonville and Caius College, died 1573.

executors or overseers : his owne hands should be executors & his eyes overseers.

Thomas Lancaster inculpe un in chauncerie pur forger & razer : le partie deny ceo : Lancaster dit le razer apiert plenement, car in veritie il vient daraine de barbour, come fut aparent :

Sept. 1598 : My L. Chief Justice in circuit : (where I was a pleder) useth to give a short exhortation & charge, touching treasons and felonies and insisting upon idle roages & other enormities in the countrey : also he is inquisitive to have espials in ech parte : and geveth a moneth before to the head constables of ech countie 12 articles to enquire & present in writing at the next assises openlie ther certificates therin : & they are to charge the petit constables in ther limits : wherby manie recusants, felones, conversion of tillage to pasturage &c. are discovered, much more than the graund Jurie do present : & upon ther certificate the graund Juries find the enditement : & if the constables or petit constables make default of *praecipe* & full presentments, fines are imposed :

Also his Lordship, upon inditement, arraynes such as are indited that they attempted rapes or burglaries, wher the fact not done to make it felonie : so if the Jurie for trial of life & death find them guiltie, they are depelie fined & bound over :

At Norwich his Lordship enveyghed against multiplicitie of sutes of vexation for petit trespasses because the grounds lie in common, advising amendes to be tendred & pleded in barre : & the plea was good *sans* doubt.

Mr. Glanville[1] now Justice gave a longe charge in Surrey omitting nothing.

In Mr. Milles[2] chamber ove Fuller,[3] Pelham,[4] Barker,[5] &

---

[1] J. C. P. June 30, 1598.

[2] William Mill : no member of Gray's Inn of that name. This is probably the Attorney and Clerk of the Star Chamber *circa* 1579-1608. (*Les Reportes del Cases in Camera Stellata*, 1593-1609, W. P. Baildon, pp. 1, 95 ; and *State Papers, Dom.*, 1598-1601, p. 57.) The office of the Clerk of the Star Chamber seems to have been in Gray's Inn. (*Pension Book of Gray's Inn*, pp. 157, 321.) At a Pension, June 19, 1588, Mr. Mill is ' allowed to sit with the Readers at their table in respect of his place and office ' (*ibid.* 81) ; and at a Pension, June 10, 1599, there is

Altam [6] : divers tales of cosenages told: especiallie of false message and tokens: & of straungers to take horses as hostellers in Inns & ride away with them: one agreed for a load of hay in Smithfield: to be delivered at Bell *alibi*: goes to the Inn-keeper at Bell and sells him the load for lesse, & takes present money: that bringes the innkeeper to Smithfield & bad the carter deliver his load to the innkeeper: & himself estopped.

Item one came to an alderman as invited guest counterfeit & took away a guilt salt, in absence of the wief, in merriment by consent of other guests : & never retorned :

Item one was rolling a packe of bed-ding downe the stairs to have stolen them : & the owner coming, he said that was the sign of the Dragon, & he went to have left the pack ther : thother told him he mistook the house like a knave, & so helped him out with his owne goodes: who was never found after.

At the L. Warden's of 5 ports [7] 50 coseners in his Lordship's livery were attending & deceved manie with false tokens & message.

One passing in the streete, a maid to whom he bad good

mention of the 'chamber where Mr. William Mill lieth adjoyninge to Graies Inn Lane on the east' (*ibid.* 143).

[3] Nicholas Fuller, admitted Gray's Inn 1563, Reader 1587 (*Gray's Inn Pension Book*, 76), Joint Treasurer 1591 (*ibid.* 500). In the first Parliaments of James I. a strong supporter of the Puritans, and employed as a lawyer to plead their cause. His defence of Ladd and Maunsell, who had suffered in the High Commission Court, caused his imprisonment in 1608. (Gardiner's *Hist.*, 1883, vol. ii. p. 40.)

[4] Edmund Pelham, admitted Gray's Inn 1563, called 1574 (*Pension Book*, 19), Reader 1588 and 1601 (*ibid.* 79, 151), Serjeant 1601, and Chief Baron Irish Exchequer 1602.

[5] Richard Barker, admitted Gray's Inn 1569 (Foster's *Gray's Inn Admission Register*, 40) ; called 1576 (*Pension Book*, 27) ; elected an *Ancient* at a Pension May 29, 1579, on the recommendation of Burghley ; see Burghley's letter, received May 26, 1579, to the Benchers, wherein it is stated that Barker had been chosen by the late Lord Keeper Bacon to be 'an instructor to his two sonnes,' when he placed them in Gray's Inn 'for the attaining of some knowledge in the studie of the lawe' (*ibid.* 37) : Reader 1594 and Joint Treasurer 1596 (*ibid.* 106, 500).

[6] James Altham, admitted Gray's Inn 1575 ; Wilbraham's 'chamber fellow' (*vide post*, August 16, 1600) ; called 1581 ; Reader 1600 (*vide post*, August 16, 1600), and Double Reader 1603 ; Serjeant 1603 ; Exchequer Baron 1606. (Foss's *Judges*.)

[7] Henry Brooke, eighth Lord Cobham.

morow was asked what he was: she answered 'Forsoth, Sir, he is Cales knight [1] by his occupation:' per Carew, Th.[2]

W[m] Gerrard said that he talking with one a yoman at Harow hill, they marvelled at the great purchases of Sir John Puckering L. keper: the yoman said 'I knew him of late in meane estate but now marvaile not at his soddaine greatnes: for it is the operacion of a L. kepership to purchase everie yere 500 pounds.'

Per Bacon *ex domino Thesaurario*: the L. of Burgaveny had morgaged that howse: the King having an ynkling therof at his meeting with him said 'God morow my L. of Burgaveny without Burgaveny': the Lord more boldlie then discretlie said to the King 'God morow my liege lord, king of Fraunce without Fraunce.'

Sir Horatio Paulo Vicino [3] Italian at Cambridge *retulit ista mihi* 1598: In purchasing landes you must consider & respect the 4 elements: 1° *terra*, the qualitie & proportionable soeing lands · 2° *aqua*, the river or other water: 3° *ignis*, how & what fuell or wood: 4° *aer* the comodious situacion for markets or dwellings · Also he saieth the nobilitie of Italie seldome wast ther patrimonie: they are so provident in ther aeconomies: in which is respect to be had to stoare up somwhat yerelie; els shall a husband be distressed once in tenne yeres by one of these 4 casualties: viz: by building: marying a daughter: sute in lawe: or service of his prince or countrey.

This 3rd of *March* 98 [4] being to see Theobalds: [5] 3 courts the

---

[1] *Cales* for Cadiz. Sixty-three knights were made there after its capture by Essex and the Lord Admiral. (*S. P. Dom.*, 1596-7, p. 263.) Essex was too profuse in his distribution of honours in Ireland also, for Chamberlain writing to Carleton, Aug. 23, 1599, mentions 59 knights made by him, and fears that 'his huddling them up by half hundreds will bring the order into contempt.' (*S. P., Dom.*, 1598-1601, p. 306.)

[2] Sir George Carew or Carey, Treasurer-at-War in Ireland.

[3] Sir Horatio Palavicino, the great merchant and political agent, passed the last years of his life at his Manor of Babraham near Cambridge, where he died in 1600. (*Dict. Nat. Bio.*)

[4] 1599.

[5] Theobalds in 1599 still belonged to the Cecils, as the exchange with the King for Hatfield was not until 1607 (Brewer's *English Studies*, p. 114). Compare a description given by Burghley, in Nichols's *Progresses of Queen Elizabeth* (vol. ii. pp. 400-3).

first for offices : the second for lodginge : wherin was the Queen's
lodging : in all that second court, the windowes beneth but one
light, those above 2 lightes without transome, and compassed at
the top : the dynyng chamber with oke, aple, chery trees : above
all the squares a large gallerie, one side all the emperors begyning
with Caesar ; thother the pictures of the chief in Europe : another
lesser gallerie with other common pictures : & 3 galleries painted
with the trees of ech shire : wherin I saw Wilbraham Coat for
Cheshire, with a half mone difference : & no such difference
in any others : & the 4 Erles of Chester since the foundation : a
fine oratorie : a little hall : a large & costlie garden : manie howses
of office : some 24 toweretts : in the Q^s chamber written over the
chymney, *Semper Adamas* : rich chymneyes &c.

5 *Aprilis* our communion sermon 1599 at Graies Inne by
Mr. Bankrout : [1] upon the text of Christ, St David & St Stephen ·
Scilicet ' in manus tuas domine commendo spiritum meum' : those
were the last words that ever Christ spake : & he upon the cross
made divers legacies : to the thief he bequethed paradize : to the
penitent forgivenes : to the obstinate damnacion : his bodie to the
crosse & his soul to God : & he saieth Christ the better to manifest
to the world the work of his passion, did choose to dye on a crosse
aloft in all mens sight, groned alowd in all men's hearing, died
in Jerusalem the greatest citie, and at the passover, being the
greatest assemblie.

The pasquill made of this pope Clement 8, was in derision of
his unworthines : viz

' Vir simplex, fortasse bonus, sed pastor ineptus :
  Ludit, agit, peragit, plurima, pauca, nihil : '

[1] I have not been able to trace this name.   The MS., besides, is a little
obscure.   On the death of Dr. Croke, several preachers seem to have been tried at
Gray's Inn ; and finally, about July 1599, Dr. Richard Fenton was elected
(*Pension Book of Gray's Inn*, p. 141).   Possibly ' Bancroft ' should be read, and
then it may be John Bancroft, nephew of Richard, the then Bishop of London.
John Bancroft, afterwards Bishop of Oxford, graduated at Oxford in 1596, and
was collated to Finchley in 1601 (Newcourt's *Repertorium*, vol. ii. p. 176).
Richard Bancroft, as rector of St. Andrew's, Holborn, 1587-97, had been closely
connected with Gray's Inn, as his church was much used by the members of the
society. (*Pension Book*, Mr. Fletcher' note p. 150.)

Yet did this pope more for the Sea of Rome then any prede-
cessores: for he recovered the dukedome of Ferrara to the Sea: &
reunited Fraunce & made 13 cardinals at one tyme: per Bacon.

22 *Apr.* 99 in private the L. ch. Justice Popham told me I
might live to see Ireland a play of 3 parties: Tirone, Butler [1] &
Florence McCharty,[2] who is chief of all the Irishrie in Mounster &
like to carry it from Ormond: tho now they be linked: this was
delivered him in secrett by the Vicont Buttevant,[3] long sithence,
to him who told her maiestie thereof: so Florence was imprisoned:
& one great councellor made to hold with him, another against
him: as it was in Condon's case:[4] & that Henry Pyne[5] that

---

[1] Thomas Butler, tenth Earl of Ormonde, in 1597 Lord Lieutenant-General of
the Forces in Ireland, and in 1599 Treasurer there for the second time.

[2] Florence McCarthy, at this time (spring 1599), had endured twelve years of
imprisonment (for the most part in London) and vain suits, his troubles with the
Government beginning in 1587, by reason of his marriage with the only daughter
and heiress of the Earl of Clancarty. (*Acts of the Privy Council*, vol. xvi. pp. 147,
381, and succeeding volumes, *passim.*) In 1595 Sir Geoffrey Fenton, Secretary
to the Council at Dublin, urges Burghley to detain Florence McCarthy, on account
of his 'Spanish affection.' (*Cal. of State Papers, Ireland*, 1592-6, p. 421.) In
April 1599 Cecil writes to Essex proposing to make use of his influence in Munster
against the rebels, and so at last his claim to the lands of the Earl of Clancarty,
in right of his wife, seems to obtain favour. (*Cal. S. P.*, Irel., 1599-1600,
p. 25.) In the same month he is in Ireland corresponding with Cecil (*ibid.* 14).
The fears of the Chief Justice, here expressed, appear to be well grounded,
for on February 29, 1600, we find Chamberlain writing to Carleton, from London,
'Florence McCarthy, lately made much of here, has fallen away in Munster
and made himself Macarty Moore, a great title in those parts, and will probably
do much harm.' (*S. P. Dom.*, 1598-1601, p. 402.) For an 'abstract of several
Treasons committed by Florence McCarthy,' see *Calendar of State Papers, Carew*,
1589-1600, pp. 514-515, and also of the reasons he 'allegeth to prove' that the
Earl of Clancarty's lands ought to descend to Ellen his wife and to her heirs, in
Carew's hand (*ibid.* 516).

[3] David FitzJames, Lord Barry, Viscount Buttevant, member of the Council in
Munster.

[4] Patrick Condon's case was against certain undertakers, who had entered on
his lands in Munster during the deputyship of Sir Henry Sidney, when Condon
was indicted and attainted of treason. (*Acts of the Privy Council*, vol. xxi. 1591,
p. 339, and vol. xxiii. 1592, p. 74.) The case dragged on, and in 1597 he had been
a suitor for nine years. (*Cal. S. P. Irel.*, 1597-8, p. 348.)

[5] 'This Patrick (Condon), being weak, was mightily backed by one Henry
Pine, of Moghelly, an English gentleman, which furnished the Spaniards with

fostered Condon was a popishe and verie daungerous fellowe : entertayner of priests, tho heare favored because he hath parteners here in the pipestaves sent for Spain.

His Lordship & I concurred, that for a sound reformation in Ireland a Parliament was necessarie to bring all lands to Englishe tenure : and to take thereby a resumpcion of all rebells' landes principals as ayders : & to such as deserved to regrant them to hold of her maiestie by small or petit reservacions : wherby all may depend upon the prince's tenure, & the certenti of the course of discent & estate knowen :

2° To be a generall disarming of the Irishrye :

3° To have a conformitie in religion, that all at lest come to churche :

also in cases of submission to tak securitie of men of foren province, that if one revolt thother may stande.

Also he told me he saw the letter written from Desmond [1] to the king of Spaine, intimating that by tyranie the Inglish had usurped upon ther lande, & so purposed to doe upon ther conscience : but he had weeded the garden better than his predecessors whose services he did remember & that he had taken the hcire aparent to the crowne ; what that ment my Lord nor I knew.

7 *Junii* 1599 : in conference with Mr. Bacon and Mr. Gerrard clerk of Duchie : we find that if all copiholders & customarie tenants were required to doble their anuall rente, & ther fines made certen for 3 lives at the lest the tenants wold assent willinglie : & it wold raize a great annuall revenue : wherby her Maiestie might pleasure manie or inrich her self: but then some great officers that had gift of stewardships, as the L. Tresorer & chauncelors of eschequer & Duchie wold loose perquisites : yet might they be better advauntaged otherwise :

also stewardes of courts of her maiestie do continew & renew copies for 3 lives : & reserve the acustomed old fines & purse up 3

---

pipe-staves. and Patrick with money, enriched himself, and forgot English sympathy.' (*Cal. S. P.*, Irel., 1599-1600, p. 499.) Sir Walter Raleigh had a grant with others for the export of pipe-staves from Munster to Spain. (*Acts of the Privy Council*, 1592-3, vol. xxiv. pp. 6, 336.)

[1] James Fitz Thomas Fitzgerald, heir of the disinherited elder son of James fourteenth Earl of Desmond. His claim to the earldom was not recognised by Elizabeth. In 1598 he joined Tyrone in rebellion.

[times] so much to ther private : and yet the ought to grent out copies of necessitie to the heires.

24 *Nov.* 99 : Patrick Crosby [1] that connyng pilot of Ireland [2] that parlied with Desmond, father Archer, legate, [3] Donogh McCragh, [4] capten Terril, [5] Mcdonogh, Knight of Kerry, [6] & used by the late president [7] as a spy, brought this : 1° that Ireland was lost & saving townes and castels all at the rebels will : that no meanes but famyne to constraine them to loyalti : & that must be by taking ther cattall and hindering the seedes & harvest and burning ther corne : that it now apereth Englishe soldiers are good onlie to garrizon & to make ˙ incursions wher they may retorne to harbour within 40 howres : & not able to make long marches nor to want ther lodginge & good diett, & that it will now troble England to send over 40,000 men which (being now unwilling to goe into Ireland) will not suffice to make recovery of Ireland : ther being 3,000 *bonoghts* in Mounster waged from

[1] Viscount Buttevant, member of the Council in Munster, writing on November 4, 1599, to Cecil, who is ' desirous to understand the certainty of all things in this kingdom and particularly in this province,' refers to Crosby thus : ' If I were to pick out one in the whole realm for that purpose I would make choice of him.' (*Cal. S. P. Irel.*, 1599–1600, p. 226.)   Elsewhere he is spoken of as, ' one that since the beginning of all these rebellions in Munster hath remained in my Lord President's house with him, and can best inform your Honour of the present state here, and the best means for reducing it to a settlement of any that I know.' (Letter of Kingsmill to Cecil, August 21, 1599, from Mallow, *ibid.* 128.)

[2] The alarming state of Ireland here described and the plan suggested for its recovery are referred to in (1) a letter from Sir Thomas Norris, President of Munster, from Cork to the Privy Council, December 9, 1598 (*Cal. S. P. Irel.*, 1598, pp. 399–400) : (2) letter of Queen Elizabeth endorsed by Cecil, ' For Munster,' wherein the information is said to come from ' our subject *P.C.*' (*i.e* Patrick Crosby), *ibid.* 1599 p. 363 ; (3) a long report, endorsed ' For Sir George Carew,' concerning the state of Ireland (*ibid.* 365–370).

[3] Father James Archer of Kilkenny, ' called the Pope's legate.' (Queen's letter *supra.*)

[4] Dr. McCragh or Creagh, ' called the Pope's Nuncio,' and ' usurped bishop of Cork.' (*Ibid.*)

[5] Captain Richard Tyrell, a rebel leader.

[6] William Fitzgerald, Knight of Kerry, ' one of the principal traitors' in Munster.

Sir Thomas Norris, late President of Munster, died of a wound on August 16, 1599, at Mallow. (*Cal. S. P. Irel.*, 1599–1600, p. 128.)

Connaght, besides all the lords & gentlemen out in Kerry : & the moste in Corke, saving Barry,[1] Roch,[2] John Fits Edmond,[3] Fynen O'Driscol,[4] Cormac McDermot,[5] Florence McCharty,[6] Donel Pipee.[7]

His plot was that Oway McRorie,[8] capten Tyrrell, & Donel Spanis[9] should invade Mounster rebels,[10] that first made them go into rebellion : & so both sides would be wasted in warre : Leinster Mounster & Connaght wold be ruyned by famyn & so made quiet : & the meane tyme the Q[s] forces to invade Ulster : 2 difficulties :

1° How Ormond wold like this, who never had any great success for us :

2° How the Irish may be allured by rewards against ther plighted vowes & religion to serve one against another : especialli against ther own allies and kindesmen : & therfore more daungerons to sett up one rebell against another in the same province : *vide lopinion de tres graund et suspected polititian evesque de Cashel*:[11] 3 leaves after.

Burghley : *Rationes in utrumque de pace seu bello cum Hispania tractatæ*, 98.[12]

Pro pace : 1° Peace most agreable with religion & civill society :
2° Her maiestie scandalized to be nurse of dissention : *ergo bone ·*
3° Commodities of peace are present, of warre future ·

---

[1] David Fitz James, Lord Barry, Viscount Buttevant.
[2] Maurice, Lord Roche, Viscount Fermoy.
[3] John Fitz Edmond, called in the Queen's letter, *supra*, ' our good old servitor.' (*Cal. S. P. Irel.*, 1599_1600, p. 363.)
[4] Fynen O'Driscoll.
[5] Cormac McDermot, chief of Muskerry.
[6] Florence McCarthy, *vide ante*, p. 24, note.
[7] *Alias* McCarthy Reogh, chief of Carberry (see *Cal. S. P. Irel.*, 1592_6, where the name is printed Na Pipi, Ne Pipee and Pypy). His wife was Desmond' sister (*ibid.*, 1599_1600, p. 364).
[8] Oway or Onie McRorie, son of Rory Oge O'Moore, chief of the Moores.
[9] Donnell Spainagh, a chief of the Kavanaghs.
[10] 'The likeliest men in Leinster are Onie McRory, Donnell Spainagh, and Captain Tyrrell. These be the men that raised all the rebellion in Munster, and these be the men that may surpress it.' (*Cal. S. P. Irel.*, 1599-1600 p. 367.)
[11] Miler Magrath, Archbishop of Cashel, 1571_1622.
[12] Camden practically gives this, *Annales Reg. Eliz.* (1627) vol. ii. p. 155 &c.

4.° Her maiestie's person more secured, if no foren enemy be to foster such assailants :

5° Great expenses wilbe avoided :

6° It is like, the warres in Ireland supported by Spaine wilbe the soner ended :

7° Traffic for the Queene and merchants reestablished to ther benefite :

8° The trade of Spain opened for bringing in money :

9° Her maiestie shall have a brething tyme to be better provided for all events

10° It may be douted whether England & Low Countreys can suport the warres ther : supress the rebellion in Ireland, & to exploit somewhat in Spaine to werie the king : and force him to better condicions.

Essex *pro bello e contra :*

1° Spaine by intermission of expence wilbe aboundantlie enriched above al princes to ther daunger :

2° Spaine will nott sitt downe with so manie dishonours & therfore no sound peace, but ever will seke revenge :

3° By peace her maiestie must abandon those of Holland & Zeland without hope of rembursement of her money disbursed for ther ayd : or els deliver the Cautionary Townes to have her money of the King of Spaine : which is more dishonorable :

4° The province destitute of the Q^s ayd shalbe made vassels to Spaine : & he thereby inabled to offend the Queene at his will & disposition.

Replicatio pro pace :

Notandum primo quod rationes pro pace validæ sunt et subsistunt, nec indigent sublevamine : & the reasons for war are thus answered :

1° Altho Spaine be inriched by peace to annoy, England by like proporcion shalbe inriched & inabled to defend :

2° The unsureness of the peace, (which is the gretest doubt) yet it is likelie the peace shall contynew : for, 1° the warre hath ben more losse to him then to England : 2° it is like the error of councellors that perswaded the king to reduce the Low Countreys to other state then his father left them, is now seene or reformed & that he will be glad to enioy them in the same manner : & 3° for the honor of revenge, proef of impossibilitie to effect & then ever appease men's passions : 4° if the Low Countreys will not be reduced by force in the meane tyme England shall gather manie advantages : also England & Fraunce united, as for politik respecte is likely they will, they shall ever be able to ballance the force of Spaine, altho he had the Low Countreys : which will not be in short time, as apereth by experience of emperor Charles, a prince of as great force & more reputacion then the king : & so England secured enoughe

3° Touching the 3 obiecion, it wilbe no reason nor fit for her maiestie to deliver the Cautionary Townes, but she may leave the protecion of the Low Countreys with honor, for her ayd was till the might have of the king reasonable condicions for ther liberti as subjects & of ther consciences in religion : for which if she be a mediator for them & they utterlie refuse, she may with honor leave them to ther own defence.

And for the loss of monie it is not to be acompted loss that hath kept the enemy so long from amongst us : & if they become obedient to Spaine, he may assent to some order for our satisfacion · if they persist in warre her maiestie may think of some other meanes for her money :

4° For the 4th reason of warre, that the king wilbe more able to annoy us : it is like the Low Countreys will not in short tyme be reduced by force : in the meane tyme manie accidents will fall out but if they be reduced by condicions of peace, they wilbe such as we shall not need to feare. for if the K. of Spain remove the army of straungers, both we & they shalbe the more secure : for the Low Countreys are like to desire the amiti of us for ther safetie : also liberti of religion being graunted, such as are so affected will have a dependency on the Queen & never be caried to any violent action against her : *quia communis necessitas facit communes amicos.* And whatsoever shalbecome of them, Fraunce & England being united, as they wilbe ever ocasioned, they shalbe a counter-poise for Spaine.

So as compare shortlie the reasons of peace & warre together :

1° The commodities of peace present, the daungers future :

2° The benefites of peace certen and sensible to be felt, the successe of warre incerten : & the suposed daunger of peace doth depend upon God & may be without daunger :

3° The peace hath in it as things now stand more ot necessitie then the warre, therfor to be preferred :

4° The good of peace to redound to England : of the warre upon others :

5° Peace avoideth blodshed : & strengtheninge of Christendom against infidels : thinge agreable to God & men :

6° reasons of warre onlie humane by presumpcions of daungers future : wherof it is better to leave the dispensation to god, founding our actions upon the rules of conscience & common good of mankind, then upon our wills conceates & suspicions to contynew courses not commendable but only by necessitie ·

the discourse it self was more enlarged.

Ultimo die termini mich. 1599 : in le star-chamber le Sieur Keper invey vers insolent libellers et presumptuouse discoursers : & abrupte vel quasi obiter declare le grand expense de royne pur preservacion de Ireland (quel sa maiestie entend seriousment a preserver) et que royne ad exhauste 30000[1] in 7 mois : et le people la plus rebellions que fuit devant : issint sa treasure mispend : car Tyrone & toutz rebels ore sont plus prowd & presumptuous de lour force que fueront devant : entant que secretarie dit que Tyrone in une darraine parlee ove Sir William Warren, dit quil ad un grand hope ore daver un share in Angleterre : & sont plusves rebels ore que fueront in marche : et les sieurs recite toutz les enterprises del Count de Essex vers les rebels, in quex chescun plusves de subiects

On the last day of Michaelmas Term 1599, in the Star Chamber, the Lord Keeper inveighs against insolent libellers and presumptuous discoursers : then abruptly and as it were by the way declares the great expense to which the Queen is put for the preservation of Ireland (which her Majesty is thoroughly determined to preserve) ; and that the Queen has exhausted £30,000 in 7 months : and that the people are more rebellious than they ever were, and so her treasure is wasted : for Tyrone and all the rebels are prouder and more presumptuous of their power than they were before : so much so that the Secretary says that Tyrone, in a parley lately held with Sir William Warren,[1] said that he had good hope to have a portion in England : and that there are more rebels now than there were in

[1] Sir William Warren held a parley with Tyrone, at the Fort of the Blackwater, towards the end of September, 1599. (*Cal. S. P. Irel.*, 1599–1600, pp. 173-4.)

fuerout occise que dez enimies : et ore tout le realme est fere al curtesie de rebels & revolt, par la negligence de governour qui ad comitt al royne errors & grand contemptes especialment in ceux pointz : viz :

1º Il etant commaund de marcher ove royall force vers rebels in Ulster in north, il (contra advise del counsell in Ireland) va ove petit army in Mounster : par que a divers skirmishes & ad le worse, al grief de subiects & encourage-ment de rebels : par que la province fuit infecte.

2º Il parle ove archtraitor Tyrone sur sute al rebel de parler ove lui, par que ils sont devenus insolent & la royne dishonore par cel private con-ference & dishonorable con-dicions, sicome sa diademe ad ete prise de luy : car ad fait ceo *precarium imperium* : & ad pro-

March.[1] The Lords also relate all the enterprises of the Earl of Essex against the rebels; in every one of which more of the Queen's subjects were slain than of the enemy : and that now the whole kingdom is at the disposal of the rebels and in re-volt, owing to the negligence of the Governor, who has com-mitted against the Queen errors and great contempts, especially in these points : viz. :

1º Being commanded to march with the Queen's army against the rebels in Ulster in the North, he (against the advice of the Council in Ireland) goes with a small force into Munster : and has divers skirmishes, wherein he has the worst, to the grief of all the Queen's subjects and the encouragement of the rebels ; whereby the province is infected.

2º He holds a parley with the archtraitor Tyrone [2] at the suit of the rebels to confer with him, whereby they are become insolent, and the Queen dis-honoured by this private con-ference and dishonourable con-ditions, as if her crown had been taken from her. For he

---

[1] Essex landed at Dublin April 14, 1599, and left Ireland September 24, 1599. A very clear account of Essex's brief span of office is given by Mr. E. G. Atkinson in the preface to the *Calendar of State Papers, Ireland,* 1599–1600.

[2] Essex met Tyrone at the Ford of Bellaclynthe, near Drumcondra, on September 7, 1599 (*Cal. S. P. Irel.,* 1599–1600, p. 146).

mise de mover la royne pur tolerance in religion.

3° Le Counte ayant licence par letter de retorne a sa volunt : uncore ce fuit countermande par autre lettre et il prohibite sur son allegeance de resider in Ireland & de pursuivre Tyrone ; tandis il a retorne in Angleterre contemptuose, & a relinquit le realm in grand perill : & sic tout le councell amplifie sur disgrace del dit counte, il estant absent, a 'son disgrace ou devant il fut repute tres haut tres noble & populer que unques fuit : *hoc audivi ab aliis.*

4 Dec 1599 : evesque de Cashel grand polititian de Ireland, et de grand experience, ayant ete ore employ par royne de parler ove toutz rebels, forque Tyrone et defery a lui : et ayant plusors conferences ove Desmond in Tower et ove Royne divers foits : dit a moy

has made her rule to depend on entreaty : and has promised to approach the Queen to give toleration in religion.

3° The Earl having license by letter to return at his will, though this license had been countermanded by another letter ordering him on his allegiance to continue in Ireland and to pursue Tyrone ; notwithstanding, has with contempt returned to England and has left the Kingdom of Ireland in great peril. And so the whole Council amplified on the disgrace of the Earl, he being absent on his disgrace, where before he was reputed most high, most noble, and popular as ever man was : this I heard from others.

4 Dec. 1599 : the Bishop of Cashel,[1] a great Irish politician, and of great experience, being now employed by the Queen to treat with all the rebels save Tyrone and to report thereon to her ; and having had several conferences with Desmond[2] in the Tower and with the

---

[1] See his letter to Cecil, dated November 15, 1599, at Westminster, offering his services to the Queen to go to Tyrone (*Cal. S. P. Irel.*, 1599-1600, p. 244) ; a Privy Council letter, dated December 2, 1599, informing the Lords Justices in Ireland that the Archbishop has Her Majesty's commission to confer with any rebels save Tyrone (*ibid.* 286-7) ; and the Archbishop's letter to Cecil, dated December 15, 1599, West Chester, where this plan is unfolded, but in less detail (*ibid.* 324-6).

[2] James Fitzgerald, the 'Tower Earl' of Desmond, for 16 years a prisoner in the Tower. In October 1600 he was sent by the Government to Ireland in the hope that the Geraldine faction would desert his rival the 'Sugan Earl' to rally round him as their genuine chief.

a son departure quil [a] licence de retorne a son plesure : et que son opinion est al royne et Sieur Montioy & Secretarie, viz. pour pacificacion de rebellion : que English soldiers ne nuques poent performe ceo: experience ad ceo declare: mes le voy est par connyng instrumentz de mitter variance et sedicion inter eux memes: et despend parcel de tresure cel voy : et quil meme est le plus apt pilott pour cel matter : entant quil est de kyune, come il pretend, al Mcguire : et Mcguire est varlet al Odorherti: et il ad alliance et creditt ove Hugh Duff Odonell et ove Oboile quex deux ont emulacion al Odonell : auxi il est grandment trusted ove Tyrone qui ad (*ut dicitur*) proclaime luy *Protector Catholice Fidei* : et son adversaries sont Tirlagh Braselagh qui est fils al Con Onele ayel al Tyrone, auxi Sir Arthure Oneyle fils al darreyne Sir Tirlagh ONeale, et Fitz Shaen Oneyle: et de exciter ceux homes de mover hostilitie vers Tyrone est le sure voy de reformacion et poet estre ore plus facile, entant que Tyrone, sil ad fait tiel insolent parlee, est desperate sans hope de pardon: ou devant nul voile relinquie luy entant quil expect que Tyrone serra les primer que serra pardone, que ore nest issint : ergo ils voile

Queen at divers times ; told me, on his departure, that he had license to return at his pleasure : and that his opinion expressed to the Queen, to Lord Mountjoy and to the Secretary, as regards the pacification of Ireland, is as follows, that English soldiers never can bring that to pass ; experience has proved this. But the way is, by means of cunning instruments, to put variance and sedition between the Irish themselves ; and in this way to spend a part of the Queen's treasure: and that he himself is the most apt pilot for this matter ; in that he is of kin, as he alleges, with Maguire ; and Maguire is a vassal of O'Dogherty : and he has alliance and credit with Hugh Duff O'Donnell and with O'Boyle, who are both the rivals of O'Donnell. Also he is greatly trusted by Tyrone, who has (as he says) proclaimed himself Protector of the Catholic Faith : and his adversaries are Tirlagh Breselagh who is the son of Con O'Neil, Tyrone's grandfather ; and Sir Arthur O'Neil, son of the late Sir Tirlagh O'Neil, and FitzShaen O'Neil : and to stir up these men to move hostilities against Tyrone is the sure way towards reformation and can be now more easily effected, seeing that Tyrone, if he has held such such *forsak him* : & purchaser favour de eux memes par service, especialment sil poent receve rewards : et 10,000 soldiers cel voy plus availe que 40,000 de Englois : et par force ou sedicion, le melior voy est de land homes soldiers al Loghfoile et il meme voile va ove eux destre instrument a mover Irishe de server vers Tyrone : come Ocane, Odoherti et auters : auxi il dit il scavoit plus de mynd de Tyrone et parle ove luy 1597, par commission : et il desire restitucion de traitors terres : et toleracion in religion pur tout Hiberniam : mais ned liberti de religion : mes destre dispunishable tanque sont couvert.

insolent parley, is desperate without hope of pardon : and where before no way was left them, seeing that they expected that Tyrone would be the first to be pardoned, it is not so now ; therefore they are willing to forsake him and purchase favour for themselves by service, especially if they can receive rewards : and 10,000 soldiers this way avail more than 40,000 English. And by force or sedition the best way is to land soldiers at Lough Foile ; and he himself is ready to go with them to be the instrument to move the Irish to serve against Tyrone, as O'Cahan, O'Dogherty, and others. Also he says that he knows most of Tyrone's mind and held parley with him in 1597 by commission : and Tyrone desires restitution of the traitor's lands, and toleration in religion for all Ireland, but not liberty of religious rites ; but to be free from punishment so long as they refrain from open religious observance.

Lancaster dit a Tanfield *Memento quod mortalis es* : etc. Est apartenant al sieur keper daver sur taker.

Hel[1] pleder dit a sieur Chancelor : que sur son honesti con science et science son allegacion fut voier : Lancaster respond quil travers touts : auterfoits il pledant dit que barganie fut *bona fide* : Lancaster pria court de granter *quo warranto* il parle latin : qui nad ete edoct ascun liberal science.

[1] Sir John Hele, of the Inner Temple : Serjeant 1594, and M.P. for Exeter 1592–1601 ; alleged to be ' drunken, insolent, and overbearing.'

Pyne[1] dit quil ne voile deliver la ley direct entant que un client sound sur counsens que son cause fut male :

Le comendacion pour royne : quel est paragon de princes : mirrhor des magistrates : admiracion a son sex : et wonder al Europe : *propugnatrix fidei.*

Ratclief dit que de vender bottle ale est le safe et spedi voie destre rich.

Contencion devant evesque de Chester[2] enter Sir Georg Beston[3] & Mr. Harvy[4] precher de Bunbury pur removing de pulpit : et Harvy excuse ceo, disant il prit cold in le pulpit pur ceo state *inter dua ostia* Beston replie ' By God, my lord, this is an idle excuse : for it was never hard that a zelous precher ever toke cold in the pulpit.'

Le royne Julii 42 regni : ad une Italian discourse le quel con teyne mil auter : forque que un magnifico in Italie ad mise un servant ove 10 chivals et 100 ova, de divers kinds, ostrech egges : egles egges, swannes egges, gese, ducks, hennes & birds egges : et quant il trove maried home que nest rule par sa feme : il donnera luy cheval : et quant il trove ascun rule par sa feme il donnera luy grand ou petit egges : acordant al supremaci de feme : et il a dispose toutz ses egges devant un cheval : al darraine apres prolixe serche il trove un disordered home nient guide par sa feme a qui il offer la choix de ses chevals : il elect gray chival, sa feme dit ' Husband, the horse with bald face is the better horse' : il mainteine son primer elecion : sa feme reioyne al contrari : et al fine prevaile issint husband desire le bald face horse : et fuit deny entant quil fut advise par sa feme.

16 *Aug* : 1600 : Wilbraham's answare being master of requests to the oration of Mr. Altham his old chamber fellowe a most lerned Reader in Graies Inn, upon 27 Eliz : ca : of errors :[5] ' Mr. Reader, the admiracion of vertue hath so depe an impression in

---

[1] John Pyne, Reader, Lincoln's Inn, 1596 (Dugdale's *Orig. Jurid.* p. 254).

[2] Richard Vaughan, 1597-1604.

[3] Sir George Beeston's monument is in Bunbury Church (Ormerod's *Hist. of Cheshire*, vol. ii. p. 263, 2nd edition).

[4] Christopher Harvey, Vicar of Bunbury, 1594_1601 (Ormerod's *Hist. of Cheshire*, vol. ii. p. 260). Bunbury was a parish in which the Puritans were very strong (*ibid.* p. 259).

[5] 27 Eliz. ca. 9 : An Act for Reformation of Errors in Fines and Recoveries &c.

nature, as filosophers do conclude, we are enforced thereby, to love those whom we never sawe, by which you may easelie coniecture with what unfained affecion we have observed you during all the tyme of your reading, which in the opinion of us all you have performed to your exceding comendacion.

' For to speke particulerlie you are the first that adventured to make a breche into this statute, which affordeth verie necessarie lerning for the practize of the lawe, especiallie in the use of pleding aknowledg worthiest to be embraced of all suche as desire to march under the ensigne of pleders. To this center you have drawen as a circumference a collecion of manie profitable question[s] of experience at the common lawe, wherein you have manifested your generall studie in all the partes of the lawe, your faithful observacion of the unprinted iudgments, your iudiciall conceates in the apt composing & lerned debating of your cases, having fixed every one of your owne rare invencions to the authoritie of some authentik & firme iudgment.

' Herin we are to acknowledg your wonderfull diligence, wherof as my self being 6 yeres your chamber fellow was an ey witnesse: so god hath geven you such fruite therof in your publik practize: as that by the best testimonie in our lawe you are consigned with the title of a lerned councellor, whereby hath redounded great honour to our societie & profitt & reputacion to your self

' Howbeit these graces I do not attribute to your lerning alone: your faithfull diligence in your clients causes, your temperate cariage in pleding, your discrete moderacion in all other your actions, by which your learning hath receved her true lustre and resplendencie, doe assuredlie promise that if you contynew in the true feare of god, & the sincere performance of your dutie in your peculiar vocacion : we shall see in short tyme his manifold blessinges infinitelie multiplied upon you to the comfort and incoragement of such as follow the same profession.

' To be short in the name of the societie I render unto you our hartiest thankfullnes, for your liberall expenses and your exceading love & paynes expressed in this exercise, wishing that as the same hath ben a loadestone to draw our attendance, so you may be a loadstarre to exalte us to the imitacion of your rare vertues : and so I conclude, out of my peculiar love, with the poet : '

[T] *bone quo virtus tua te vocat; i pede fausto.*

Peroratio si amplificata.

Tu regere imperio populos, Regina, memento:
Hae tibi artes erunt pacisque imponere morem.

The Printer was a loser by his first impression of Rables · then he caused a precher in his sermon to inveigh against the vanitie therof: since which it hath ben 6 tymes under presse: so much it was in request.

Yong Christopher Swifte refused a challeng of old Sir Georg Beston: saying he wold not geve Beston so much advantage to venture, a lief of 60 yeres to Beston's of three yeres.[1] The amner [2] in his sermon upon the Queen's nativiti day, said, her health is our solace: her ioy our tryumphe: her lief our preservacion: for if she grieve we morne: if she be sick we languish: if she dye we perishe.

14 *Jan*: 1600[3] ieo fui present al councell ou tres graund consultacion fuit pur abasement de coyne pour Ireland: issint que lexpences le roy in vanquishant les traitors poet estre contynewe:

primo fuit agree que embasement de coyne inhaunce le price de touts merchandize, foren especiall: et auxi de vittails et touts auters choses ·

2º. Fuit agree que soldier que receve ce paie serra distresse et discontent:

3º. Que ce induce barbarisme et idlenes in ce realme: come

14 *Jan.* 1600. I was present at the Council, where there was great consultation touching the debasement of the Irish coin: in order that the expenses of the Queen in vanquishing the traitors may be maintained.

First it was agreed that debasement [4] of coin enhances the price of all merchandise, especially foreign merchandise: and also of victuals and everything else.

2. It was agreed that soldiers receiving their pay in debased coin will be distressed and discontented.

3. That this causes barbarism and idleness in this realme: as

---

[1] Sir George Beeston died in 1601, aged 102 (see his monument in Bunbury Church as given by Ormerod in his *History of Cheshire*, vol. ii. p. 263).

[2] Dr. Anthony Watson, bishop of Chichester, appointed Queen's Almoner about 1595. (*Dic. Nat. Bio.*) [3] 1601.

[4] For a summary of this policy of debasing the Irish coinage, see Gard. *Hist.* vol. i. p. 365·

fut devant le coyne refine : car nul artificer fuit fere in Ireland devant :

4°. Ore vient in question et fere resolue par touts que le auncients coigns doent estre descrie, et disanul par proclamation : ou auterment ceo base coyne ne serra regard ne accept in contracts ·

5°. Donque fere resolue que le auncient standerd dengleterre fuit que pur un pound weight de silver serra 12 ounces : dont 11 ounces et 2^d weight serra pure : et lauter 18^d weight serra de alloy : et que temps E 3 : xxd fuit un ounce de silver : mes apres temps H 8 : fuit semel raise al 2^s 6^d le ounce par proclamation : et sic par proclamation estre par degrees raise al vs le ounce weight :

6°. Il semble que franktenants quex ont terres in demesne, ou terres dont ils poent improve les rents, ne serra damnifie mult par abasement : pur ceo ils poent doble et treble lour rents. Mes pensioners, captens, soldiers, et touts quex vivent sur certen rents serra grandement damnifie, et mult discontent :

7°. Ils agree que si ascun course deschaunge poet etre

was the case before the coin was reformed : for there was no artificer in Ireland before that time.

4. Then the question arose, and it was resolved by all that the old coin must be decried and disannulled by proclamation ; or otherwise that base coin will not be regarded or accepted in contracts.

5. Then it was resolved that the ancient standard of England was that in one pound weight of silver there should be twelve ounces : whereof 11 oz. 2 dwt. should be pure and the remaining 18 dwt. should be alloy : and that in the reign of Edward III the value of one ounce of silver was 1s. 8d., but afterwards in the reign of Henry VIII the value of the ounce was raised, at first, to 2s. 6d., by proclamation : and so to be raised by degrees by proclamation to 5s. the ounce.

6. It seems that freedholders who have lands in demesne, or lands whereof they can raise the rent, will not suffer much harm by the debasement, because they can double and treble their rents ; but pensioners, officers, soldiers, and all who live by certain rents will be greatly harmed and exceedingly discontented.

7. They agree that if any system of exchange can be

que soldiers serra releve, et rebels sustendera le losse dabasement ceo hasten le peace, par lour povertie : al fine semble destre resolue par touts que ob : & 1^d serra coyne de basse metall tout ousterment : et que 3^d vi^d et xii^d serra coine de 3 ounces fine et 9 ounces alloy : issint que serra 3 parts base et 4 part pure : et que novel stampe serra devise, a coyner 100,000 pour service de Ireland *tantum* : et que touts auters coynes la currant serra decry, et disanul : issint que tout retorner in Engleterre :

Et donque Tresorer de Ireland promise que ascun merchants undertake de aver eschaunge de donner a chesoun soldier ou subiect, sterling pur ceo base Irishe : pur 2^s in 20^s losse in exchaunge : et ceo il performe sans damag al royne plus que 50,000 [1] : car cy tost que ce vient destre eschaunge, il voile utter ceo al army arere : et sic il uttera ceo sans losse ouster 50,000 *initio*.

In ce case devant un caution doet etre que nul counterfett ce base coyne : et par ce voi le

effected, so that the soldiers shall be relieved and the rebels bear the loss occasioned by the debasement of the coin, it will hasten peace by reason of the poverty of the rebels. In conclusion it seems to be resolved by all that the penny and halfpenny shall be coins of base metal entirely, and threepences, sixpences, and shillings shall be coined, whereof three ounces shall be pure and nine ounces alloy; so that there be three parts base and the fourth part pure; and that a new stamp shall be devised to coin 100,000 for the service of Ireland only: and that all other coins current there shall be decried and disannulled, so that all shall return to England.

And then the Treasurer of Ireland promises that some merchants shall undertake to provide exchange to each soldier or subject, sterling for debased Irish coin, at a loss of two shillings for every pound in exchange : and that he will effect this without loss to the Queen, saving one of £50,000 : for as soon as the debased Irish coin comes to be exchanged he will issue it back again to the army : and so he will issue it without loss, saving the £50,000 in the first instance.

In this case precaution must first be taken that no one shall counterfeit this debased coin:

royne doet eschaung infinite somes a son detriment : et par case serra bone sur chesoun issue daver bill endented et sic de reprender ce par eschaunge, par que le rebell serra prevent.

Eschange est devise (come apiert in *statuts de money* temps E. 3, et par que eschaung fuit pur bullion daver silver et pur un coyne daver auter :) que ceux de Ireland qúe aport baze coyne aver sterling in Angleterre, ove losse de 2^s in 20^s : et ceux quex deliver bone coyne in Ireland aver baze la et le 7 part plus : come $23^s 4^d$ pour 20^s bone silver : et uncore par le doble treble et sextible uttering de base in Ireland (plus que lauter eschaunge desire al benefite de subiect) la royne gainira multe : *vide* Rastel, *titulo Eschaunge*. 25 E. 3 ca. 12 : 14 R. 2 ca. 2. et 3 H. 7 ca. 6, eschaunges forbidden but by the King's license & officers : which semes foren eschaunges.

5 E. 6 ca. 19 *ibid* : no man

and thus the Queen should have to exchange infinite sums to her detriment : and perhaps it will be a good plan on each issue to have an indented bill, and so to take the bill back again in exchange : and in this way the rebels will be prevented.

Exchange was devised, as it appears, by a statute relating to money in the reign of Edward III, whereby exchange was to afford silver for bullion : and for one coin to have another that those of Ireland who brought debased coin should have sterling in England, at a loss of two shillings in the pound : and those who deliver good coin in Ireland should have debased coin there and a one seventh in addition : for instance 23s. 4d. for 20s. good silver : and yet by the double treble and sextuple issue of debased coin in Ireland (more than the other exchange desires with benefit to the subject) the Queen will gain much. See Rastall, title ' Exchange.' [1] 25 Edward III ca. 12, 14 Ric. II ca. 2, and 3 Henry VII ca. 6, forbids exchange unless by the King's license, and through his officers ; this seems to refer only to foreign exchange.

5 Edward VI. ca. 19 *ibid.* : no

---

[1] William Rastall, J.Q.B. 1558_1562. The references are to his collection of all the statutes from _Magna Charta_ to *1, Elizabeth,* arranged under their subjects in alphabetical order.

shall take for eschaunge of gold for silver any profitt, above the rate, *pena* forfeture :

19 Henry 7 : ca. 5, R. *money* 45 : nul argent doet etre cary dengleterre al Ireland : nec de Ireland al Ingland *pena* forfeture.

Temps E. 3, etc : divers statutes quex prohibit transportacion de ascun silver, gold, bullion, plate, hors de realme : et ascun statute prohibite que nul serra port transmare in Engleterre : semble le reason fuit pur ceo notre coyne fuit plus pure que lauter.

Auxi apiert par statute E. 3 : que Galli halfpence et Scottishe coyne fuit abase in lour price in Engleterre de temps in temps come le coyne fuit abase in puritie in Engleterre.

man shall take, in exchanging gold for silver, any profit above the lawful rate, under pain of forfeiture. 19 Henry VII. ca. 5, Rastall, ' Money,' 45. No silver is to be carried from England to Ireland or from Ireland to England under pain of forfeiture. *Temp.* Edward III. etc. : divers statutes which prohibit transportation of any silver, gold, bullion or plate out of the realm : and some statutes ordain that no one shall bring coin over sea to England. The reason for this seems to be that our coin was purer than other coin.

Also it appears by a statute of Edward III. that Galley-halfpennies and Scotch coin were debased in their value in England from time to time, as the coin was debased in purity in England.

Parliament terme Mich. 43 et 44 R^{ac} fuit dissolve 19 Dec. 1601.[1]

Crook recorder de Londres apres que la royne fuit in sa royal throne, fuit conduct al barre par 2 councellors de lower howse : & apres 3 humble congees & silence, il fit oration a cel effect.

' Most sacred prince & renowned soveraigne : man cannot live without societie, no societie can contynew without order, no order without lawes which are the bonds & ornaments of all societie.

' The highest above all lawes and law makers first ingraved lawes in man's harte to discerne good from evell, to embrace the one & eschew the other : after when vice increased lawes were

---

[1] In the Reports of Townshend (pp. 149–151) and D'Ewes (pp. 618–9) the speeches of the Speaker and the Lord Keeper are far less fully given than here, while the Queen's speech is entirely omitted.

ordeined to protect the good & correct the evell. But sithence
the mutabilitie of all thinges had predominance in men's actions,
the lawes established must be varied & made aplicable to the
infinite diversitie of circumstances.' In lawes & government he
said religion was *primum, secundum & tercium* : & that all her
maiestie's lawes (according to the divine inspiracion of her sacred
spirite) tended evermore to the establishment of sincere religion,
wherein her royall hart was firmely fixed : & therfore no doubt
but wold fructifie to her immortal praise & the prosperitie of her
people.

2°. Secondlie, he declared that the Lords & Commons assembled
had considered of divers publik & private lawes, which now
gaspe for brethe from your all powerfull Maiestie who onlie can
geve them lief. Her maiestie's lawes are the limbes of iustice
tending to the continuance of our happie peace : & it maie not
be said of them, *Dat veniam corvis, vexat censura columbas* : he
praised our happie peace & praied we might long enjoy it under
her.

3°. Thirdlie he shewed that an honorable councellor, member of
the lower howse, had declared to them that Spaine & Rome had
conspired against her Maiestie his annointed & absolved them of
Ireland from allegeance & thundred all possible threates against
such as persisted in ther loyaltie : they had sent wolves amongst
her Maiestie's subiects, some like lions in force of armes to compell,
some like lammes by pretence of puritie of religion which was
idolatrie to seduce them from ther due obedience.

But ther curses shall retorne upon themselves & they shalbe
intrapped in ther owne snares ; for god will ever preserve his
anointed because her royall hart hathe never started from his holy
hestes : for the better preparacion against these cruell foes, the
Lords & Commons considering the great charges exhausted in the
iust defence of her people have most humblie & willinglie (& then
made low conges) presented to her maiestie 4 subsidies & 8
fiftenths & tenths, in token of there zelous hartes (tho not equall
to the charges), who are evermore redi to sprinkle ther hart bloude
in their enimies faces, for the service of her maiestie.

4°. He rendred all humble thanks for her maiestie's most ample
gracious and free pardon, commending her iustice to be admirable,
so her mercy to be most renowned and magnified to all posteritie :
lastlie he craved pardon, for his weeknes, infirmitie & oversights,

especiallie in his defections, relating to the howse her maiestie's gracious favours espressed by her towards them in such divine & supernaturall manner, as his weeknes could not undergo so high & weighti a charge : but desired upon his knees that *voluntas reputabitur pro facto* : & so ended.

The Lord Keeper called to the Queen : & she delivered him in secret charge what to answere : who retorning to his place said to this effect (both orations held about one howre & no more :)

' Mr. Speaker the Q^s most excellent Maiestie hath hard & considered your grave & lerned speche, & commanded me to signifie her gracious pleasure to ech part of your spech, a charge to hevi for me to undergoe.

' Touching the first part of your spech concerning the praise & necessitie of lawes, her Maiestie geveth all approbacion : especiallie in your conclusion wher you acknowledge that therin & in all her government she hath evermore knitt them to sinceritie of religion : for without that she disdaines all praise of other vertues, *quæ splendescunt subtilitate & franguntur vanitate.*

' Touching your lawes made, she findes more private lawes than publick : whereby the charge imposed in the begyning of parliament hath not ben observed : & tyme might better have ben spent in publick, but therein she notes private respects are carried in publick affairs which ought not to be.

' Concerning your 4 subsidies & 8 fiftenth & x^{ths}, presented for the warres, she acknowledges the loving bountie of her subiects to be extraordinario : but the like cause of expense of treasure was never before : & her maiestie doth take the manner of free geving without grudging, & to be geven in the beginning of the parliament, as thankfullie as the gifte : & tho she accept it as a gift to herself, yet she requireth you & all her subiects to knowe that she hath never ben gredie gryper nor covetous keper, contemning ever more welth without honor : this bountie of her subiects is not to spare or supplie her royall expenses, but in part of the charges bestowed for ther defence, whereof her maiestie is so dearlie affectionate, that she hath sold & doth still sell of her auncient inheritance for the defence of her so liberall & loving subiects; & this subsidie her maiestie challengeth no use or propertie but the troble of distribucion : & sithence her maiestie is so graciouslie thankfull for the subsidie, she expecteth that the Lords & Commons will show example from themselves of inst

taxacion : & so by example excite others that it maie be as large in
deeds as in wordes :

'Her maiestie geveth you all great thanks for your discret
carriage in debate of your councells in this parliament: & in
especiall because in every occurrance that aymed at her prerogative,
which she preserveth to the good of her subiects & the offence of
none, you preserved the same by petition to her sacred person :
obedience better then sacrifice : she nedeth non that cannot obey
as of law : Essex.

'Her maiestie hath graunted them a gracious and liberall
pardon : & she well understandeth what she hath geven and
remitted them, whereby her bountie is more to be honored : her
sword of Justice never shineth more then oyled with mercy.

'And lastlie to you Mr. Speker she not onlie thinketh you worthy
of pardon but geveth you great thanks for your wise & discret
cariage : acknowledging your deserts equal with any your predecessors.'

All charged to repaire to the countrey & not to winter in
London like butterflies spend summer abrod : that the Justices of
peace be vigilant & not drones, nor quarelous champertors.

The Parliament being dissolved & ech one redie to depart
without further expectacion as the manner is, the Queen's
Maiestie raised herself out of her royal seate & made a short, pithie,
eloquent & comfortable spech somewhat to this effect : [1] for besides
I could not well heare all she spake, the grace of pronunciacion &
of her apt & refined wordes so lernedlie composed did ravish the
sense of the herers with such admiracion as every new sentence
made me half forget the precedents.

'My Lords, we have thought it expedient in this general

---

[1] This fine speech of the Queen is not even mentioned in the Parliamentary
Reports, nor have I been able to find any report of it elsewhere.   Carleton, however,
in a letter dated London, December 29, 1601, to Chamberlain, writes : 'The
Parliament ended on Saturday seven night.   I was present as a burgess, and
heard good counter-clawing and interchangeable flattery between the Speaker and
my Lord Keeper in behalf of the Queen.   The Queen concluded all with a long
speech, which was much commended by all those who heard her : the Bishop of
Durham told me he had never heard her in a better vein.'   (S. P. Dom.,
1601-3, p. 134.)

assemblie to lett you know out of our owne mouth the unfayned attestacion of our hart.

'First we humblie acknowledg the innumerable & unspekable benefits of Almighty God for our miraculous preservacion from the traitorous practises of miscreant subiects who, designed thereto by foren enimies, have sought by taking away our lief, (which we are ever most willing to render up to him that gave it) have sought therby to bring our people & kingdome, (being farre more deare to us then our owne lief) into perpetuall thraldome & foren tiranie.

'And to saie the truthe ther have ben so manie & divers strata-gems & malicious practises & devises to surprise us of our lief, as in recording therof I am forced to recognize the mercyes & omni-potencie of the eternall God, by whose providence I have escaped all ther snares, & some of the malefactors sentenced to perpetuall shame & deserved punishment.

'The nomber of these wicked complotters, the severall manners of undertaking therof, & how some of them were discovered before the came to ther ripenes, other brought forth abortive, some others even in ther full maturitie extinguished, it were to small purpose particulerlie now to recount; ther be divers gentlemen our ministers that can redelie testifie the truthe & circumstances hereof. Our purpose onlie is to acknowledge our constant & irre-movable dependencie upon his mereyes by whose goodnes we that trust ever in him have ever ben preserved.

'Next you shall understand that touching our civill government, sithence the begyning of our raigne, in all causes we have under-taken to heare & determyne, our hart hath ben as a playne table redie to receave any impression: so most willing to heare the allegacions of ech partie, yet evermore inclining our sentence to the sinceritie of proef & soundnes of reason.

'Touching our affaires with foren princes I must discover some things not knowen to many, and those of our Councell in the secrecy of our state. In the begyning of our raigne those of the Low Countreys presented manie peticions to us & our neighbour princes to be protected against inquisitioners of Spaine & other opresions not sufferable, wherein we remembering the auncient amytie be-tween our predecessors & the howse of Burgundie, & knowing how farre Spaine was remote from the Low Countreys & fearing his soldiers revolt ther for want, sent pay to them to conteyne them,

& advertised the King of Spaine, by twelve persons severallie at the lest : that if he did not loose the raigne in easing the Lowe Countreys from ther over hevi burdens, they were redie & likelie to seek their protecion from other foren princes to his harme & dishonor. But this potent prince, (whose sowle I trust is with God, howsoever his demerites have bene towards us) not regarding our advise, continued still in extremities : which forced those people to seek & sue for our protecion by manie peticions, & in ther owne wisdome finding our inclination inseparablie knitt to contynew the former amitie with Spaine, they shewed us the severall instruments wherby the king & the emperor his father were sworn (a strange oath for kinges) that if those subiects did not enioy the ymmunities therin promised them the might lawfullie seek protecion of any other prince : exciting us out of our compassionate disposicion to relieve ther knowen extremities. Upon which we graunted them some defence, onlie till by our mediacion or process of tyme some moderacion might be founde, which we thought was required in christianiti & yet no brech of amitie : but the late king (before this) in recompense of our princelie kindnes towards him in our former advertisement & lones, excited a daungerouse rebellion in the north by the earles of Northumberland & Westmoreland, which being quicklie & happelie extinguished, he still contynewed all malicious courses, I neede not say of attemptes of invacion but the invacion it self which by God's potencie was defeated. And now the yong king [1] following his father in malice will begynne it semes warre upon us : when it is well knowen that we have often refused the resignacion of the Low Countreys (which the Archduke hath) into our protecion, (a great temptacion to any prince to be soveraigne over so rich a people) being led therto by a desire not to infringe in any point that former amitie, & especiallie desiring an established prosperitie & peace to our people rather then any enlargement to our owne honour. This we speak to lett you & all others knowe this warre is causeless, not drawen upon us by anie provocacion of ours, but a rashe enterprise, proceding of malice or vaine glorie : wherby as we nothing feare, so lett no man doubt but that the iustice & omnipotence of God is such, that in every warre he geveth victorie to the innocent, & fighteth evermore for those that sincerelie serve him : upon which confidence we may

[1] Philip III. became king in 1598; in 1601 he was twenty-three years of age.

repose our selves in corage & alacritie, whatsoever be practized against us. Concerning our affecion to our people, it is our happiest felecitie & most inward ioy, that no prince ever governed a more faithfull valiant & loving people : whose peace & prosperitie we evermore preferre before all temporall blessinges : & be you well assured whether we mak peace or warre, the good of our people shalbe evermore preferred therin. We never attempted any thinge to damage or dishonour our people & tho we may not attribute merites to our owne witt in chosing out the safest harbour for us all to ancor at : yet the finger of God, directing the actions of all princes that sincerely serve him, & our long lived experience, tho in a meane witt, shall mak us able to discerne & embrace that which shall tend to the prosperitie of our people : to whom I wishe, that they that wishe them best may never wishe in vain.'

In the upper parliament hangings, amongest other emblems, the embleme of raging love is sett in the arays with these 2 verses :

Cura placens, predulce malum, tristisque voluptas ·
Heu vesana furens pectora vexat amor.

26 *Jan.* 1601 : her majestie commaunded me to deliver this message to the lord Maior [1] : first she marveled he did not proceade with the erecion of an hospitall for relief of pore at 300*l. per annum*, entended & agreed on by his predecessor : secondlie requiring him to cause restraint of the vagarant roagues about London : & to retorne his private answare.

His Lordship, 27 *Jan.* 1601 ; desired me retorne this answare to the first : that the aldermen denied anie such conclusion to have ben : & that latelie at the instance of the chief Justice, his Lordship & the aldermen had labored therin, but could not perswade it by reason of other great charges happening of late which yet are not collected : namelie 4,000*l.* paid for 2 gallies, 18 soldiers (*sic*) sent to Ostend, others to Ireland : that Bridewell geven to so good a purpose by E. 6, was now made a prison & so spent much that way : & that Surrey & Middlesex, for whom this relief was chieflie, should provide for ther owne.

To the second : he said he found the constables & sidemen negligent, & he confessed the fault of his remisenes but it should

[1] Robert Lee.

be redressed : onlie he found the pore so manie & distressed that some convenience must be for begars or els they wold starve.

Wilbraham's spech being Master of Requests to seriant Pelham for his farewell in Graies Inne hall, *Nov*: 1601 : being called seriant to thentent to be Chief baron in Ireland : & in answare to the seriant.

' Mr. Seriant we do all excedinglie reioice to see vertue is worthelie honored, in a gentleman so beloved in this societie.

Your humble recognizion to her Maiestie that so graciouslie hath called you to this preferment doth argue to the world that being so unfainedlie thankfull to acknowledg, you wilbe seriouslie intentive to deserve this highe favor.

' For your gratefull ennumeracion of benefitz ascribed to this societie, we cannot but commend your humilitie being the proper ensigne to all your vertues, & embrace your love out of our best affecions, promising that as your advauncement hath geven honor to our felowship, so shall our assistance be evermore redie to improve your fortunes.

' God graunt that this your dignitie raised out of vertue, may be a day dawning starre to geve light & example to others by like desert to mount into the same sphere.

' It were presumpcion to advise you in any thing : yet we in kindnes of good will may entreate you to call to mynd that in this plentifull harvest of pleders you are selected to the highest dignitie incident to your calling. Remember therfore you are placed as a probacioner in an open theatre to this end that if by publick triall you shall aprove & as I hope increse the opinion of your lerning & sinceritie in this ministeriall function : you may heareafter be advaunced to magistracie of weightie imployment for the service of your prince & good of your countrey.

' Forgett not then these short memorialls : first that the grace procedeth from God, the bountie from a soveraign prince, the meanes hath ben the comendacion of frends : but the merite hath growen out of your owne vertues.

' Therfore to conclude, be you of good corage, put on in God's name all sailes, & now shew your self a circumspect pilott. We will wish you evermore a prosperous wynd, & that the haven which is in your kennyng may prove a happie harbour for you to ancor at : *finis.*' [After in *Aug.* he was chosen Chief baron for Ireland.]

24 *Maii*, 1602 : the Lords of Councell falling in spech of the great exhaust of 180,000*l.*, these last 7 yeres warres, & that the charge now was of Irish warres, being 19,000, viz. nynteene thowsand in pay was 400,000*l.*[1] *per annum*, & that the treasure & men of England being wasted, it was not to be endured : & that potts & pewter were selling amongest the pore for this present subsidie.

The Lords seemed to agree it was the Irish warres had impoverished England, & not the warres of Spain or Low Countreys : & if the Queen had the treasure spent in Ireland they all agreed we should contynew warre with Spaine.

They all agreed the Low Countreys will never become subiects, to Spaine or Fraunce or any other : but will maynteyne a contynuall warre. And therein are able by strength of the fortificacions & townes to werie Spaine & Fraunce : with our ayd of men especiallie.

They also agree that we may not with any safetye suffer Spaine or the Arch Duke to be absolute in the Low Countreys : for therby our daunger were farre more.

That point excepted if we might contynewe amitie with the Low Countreys, peace with Spaine were to be embraced : *rebus sic stantibus*.

But they were devided touching peace to be moved by us with Spaine : for the Lord Tresurer said, the warre in the Low Countreys was not to end the cause but a lingering warre to waste us & them : & that it was fittest to have peace with Spaine before we be to farre spent : for he hath a spring that yeldeth contynuall supplie, his Indies : & we are like a standing water, which warre will exhaust & mak drie & barren : & the maintenance of those rebels is to wast England : & wished a tretie but wold desparre the execution (?) now for ever.

The Lord Admirall Mr. Controller[2] & Mr. Secretarie *contra*, first to be moved by us were her maiestie's dishonor, yet they wold be content a treatie might be moved from them : some good might arize by gayning tyme.

[1] A list of the army as it stood on January 1, 1603, gives a total of 13,100 men (*Cal. of State Papers*, *Carew*, 1601-3, pp. 396-8) ; while in a statement bearing date March 31, 1602, from the 'Treasurers' accounts,' the entertainment of the army in Ireland from April 1, 1601, to March 31, 1602, 'The Lord Mountjoy being Lord Deputy,' amounts to 322,502*l.* 0*s.* 1¼*d.* (*ibid.* p. 504).

[2] Sir William Knollys, to Dec. 1602 (*S. P. Dom.* 1601-3, p. 271).

Secondlie ther is no amitie firme amongest princes but as serves ther common weales, wherof they have government: & therfore Spaine & Praunce are now in no better termes almost, but as before the peace.

Thirdlie no safetie to have peace with Spaine, for that the Enfanta makes title of succession.

Lastlie & chieflie if we should conclude peace with Spaine all agree we must secretlie ayd the Lowe Countreys against them · in requitall whereof they have & will ayd the rebels in Ireland · so the peace of no availe to us: if we have such warres in Ireland, we weare as good to have it with Spaine: but if peace were with the rebels ther, (as M[r] Secretarie said every good councellor wold advise) then wold our condicions of peace with Spaine be more honorable & beneficiall.

But the Lord Tresurer replyed that if an outward peace were with Spaine, the rebels wold submitt themselves to any condicions: & tho the peace break after, we should gaine advantage of tyme & treasure, the wast wherof is unsupportable.

The Lord Keper, Erle of Worcester & M[r] Secretarie Herbert were silent all this round disputacion: & so they rose from the table, non wayting ther but myself & M[r] Wade:[1] some say we take no harm by some warre, to wast idle: *quaere hic antea*, reasons *utrinque* for warre or peace.

29 *Aug.* 1602: At the court at Otelands: the lord Ever,[2] secretarie Herbert, doctor Dun,[3] sworne late Master of Requests for this service, & M[r] Leasure,[4] did tak the leave of the Queen: & at the councell table (they being ambassadors for Denmark) ther were read & delivered to them certen provisional instrucions to treat with the Emperour (if he desired it) as was suposed, touching

---

[1] Clerk of the Council.

[2] Ralph, third Lord Eure or Evre, Vice-President of the Council of the North (*S. P. Dom.* 1601_3, p. 155).

[3] Sir David Dun or Donne.

[4] Sir Stephen Le Sieur. On June 17, 1603, payment is made out of the Exchequer to ' Master Stephen Le Sieur,' lately sent as assistant to the ambassadors of her late Majesty on a mission to the King of Denmark (Devon's *Exchequer Issues*, p. 3). He was knighted in 1608 (Metcalfe's *Book of Knights*, p. 159), and naturalised in 1624 (*Statutes at Large*, 21 James I., Private Acts, Table of Contents; see also *Dict. Nat. Bio.*)

our commerce within his territories, & the reallowing the liberties of the Hans Townes, within England.[1]

The somme is: first, they to have fredome, as English, to transport woll & cloth the chief trade to the Empire onlie: & to bring ther countrey commodities to us as free as English: but if the bring foren commodities, to pay custome as strangers: & to have the Stilliard howse allotted to them: as it hath ben.

And we *contra* to have some citie in Germaine for our merchants to trade our wolle & clothe to: being as is agreed the welth of England.

But note Mr Secretarie Cecyll hath divers treaties wherby H. 7, after King E. 6, Q. Marie, disanulled the great liberties of the Hans Townes in England: for that they colored stranger's goods: & by merchandizing our cloth into the Low Countreys deprived the gaine of our merchants: but the liberties in part were regraunted by her maiestie: & after, upon ther abuses, resumed & they sent away: & this hoped colloquie may renew the amitie & intercourse of traffick to the good of them both.

Sieur ch. Justice dit a moy, que in Condons case, doubtfull subiect de Ireland, pollicie fuit que Sr Tresorer serra adverse a son sute pur restitucion de son terre attaint: & s^r chauncelor serra pur luy: et doctor Swale, un mynion al dit chauncelor Hatton, dit a moy que fuit pollicie que sieur chauncelor serra adverse a Sr John Perrot: et sieur Tresorer pur luy ut amy pur faire luy daver iustice: et	The Lord Chief Justice told me that in Condon's[2] case, an Irish subject whose loyalty was in suspicion, the plan was that the Lord Treasurer should be opposed to his suit for the restitution of his attainted land, and the Lord Chancellor for him. And Dr. Swale,[3] a creature of the said Chancellor Hatton, told me that the plan was that the Lord Chancellor should be opposed to Sir John Perrot,[4] and

---

[1] For this embassy see *S. P. Dom.* 1601-3, p. 246, Chamberlain to Carleton.

[2] *Vide ante*, p. 24.

[3] Richard Swale, civilian, President of Caius College, Cambridge, appointed in 1587 a Master of Chancery through the influence of Sir Christopher Hatton, who is said to have relied on his legal knowledge for guidance in the discharge of his duties as Lord Chancellor. (*Dict. Nat. Bio.*)

[4] Lord Deputy of Ireland 1584-91. Recalled and tried for high treason, he was

tamen ils entend un fyne, que loffender aver son desert.

the Lord Treasurer for him as a friend desirous to gain him justice; and yet it was understood between them that there should be a fine and the offender was to meet with his deserts.

Episcopus London, *camera stellata*: *febr.* 1602, dit que sur examinacion de Jesuitz & seculer priestz, ils confesse periurie destre allowe pur catholicks in Angleterre: quia dicunt quod papa Pius Quintus excommunicavit Reginam Elizabeth: par que toutz ses magistrates & lour authoritie sont adnihilate; et donques lour text est: *Juramentum coram iudice non competente non obligat*: sic il dit ils teyne destre loyall pur catholiks de cosen toutz protestantz de lour bargaines & dettry.

The Bishop of London, in the Star Chamber, February 160⅔, said that Jesuits and secular priests confessed, on examination, that perjury was lawful for Catholics in England, because they say that Pope Pius V. has excommunicated Queen Elizabeth; and so all her magistrates and their authority are annihilated. And their text is, an oath taken before a judge illegally appointed is not binding: so he says they hold it lawful for Catholics to cozen all Protestants in bargains and debts.

Auxi apiert que evesque London par advize Councell, et come il dit a moi, de secretarie especialment, ad travaile de faire discord enter Jesuitz & seculer priest: par que ils ont escrit divers railinge quodlibetz & pampheletz lun vers auter: par

Also it appears that the Bishop of London, on the advice of the Council, and, as he told me, especially by the Secretary's advice, has worked to bring about discord between the Jesuits and the secular priests, whereby they have written di-

---

found guilty on very insufficient evidence. He died in prison in September 1592. Thomas Phelippes writes, March 22, 1591: 'Sir John Perrot was committed to the Tower. . . . There is a diversity of opinion respecting him, as men are diversely inclined to the Chancellor or the Lord Treasurer, who was said to be sick when Perrot was sent to the Tower, and has not left his chamber since. . . . The Earl of Essex [favours him] . . . but the Chancellor has great dependency, and if his proofs are as evident as the accusations are odious they will weigh all down.' (*S. P. Dom.* 1591-4, p. 21.)

que le traitorous purpose de Jesuitz pur deposer le roy come illoyal ad apere de lour escriptures de memes : auxi in lour apelle al Rome lun vers lauter, ils recede a pape discontent : le Jesuite que ad le countenaunce de Spaine totaliter, pur ceo le seculer ne sont reiect : le seculer pur ceo nont melior allowance : sed uno ore consensi sunt re vera advers protestantz, coment le writings voile colour le contrari, come episcopus et secretar dicunt & credunt.

vers railing quodlibets and pamphlets against one another, so that the treacherous purpose of the Jesuits to depose the Queen as unlawful has appeared from their very writings. Also, in their appeal to Rome against each other,[1] they left the Pope discontented—the Jesuits, who have the countenance of Spain entirely, because the plea of the secular priests was not rejected; the seculars because they are not more countenanced. But with one voice they are in reality in agreement against the Protestants, however their writings would imply the contrary, as the Bishop and secretary say and believe.

Referunt nonulli, quod Dominus Custos Sigilli[2] pro vale al seriant Hele,[3] dixit, ' god be with you Mr Seriant & prosper you in the Tribe of Isacar : ' le quel Heale ne perceve : mes sur serch de ses amies ils trove que Genesis ca. 49,[4] that Isacar was betwene twoe burdens & to serve for tribute, ut Jurisperiti solent.

Nota 20 *marcii*, 1602:[5] After Queue Elizabeth had languished 3 wekes, to all seming rather of torment of myud then payne of bodie, & refusing all phisick, after dailie and maniefold stronge exhortacions, both by bishops and the Councell, not to be her owne ruyue : against this day was a sommons of all the bishops

---

[1] For this appeal to the Pope see a letter of Thomas Phelippes to Cecil November 3, 1602 (*S. P. Dom.* 1601-3. p. 254), and the Pope's bull to Blackwell the Archpriest, $\frac{\text{Sept. 25}}{\text{Oct. 5}}$, 1602 (*ibid.* pp. 257-8).

[2] Lord Keeper Egerton.

[3] John Hele, of the Inner Temple ; called to the Bar 1574 ; to the Bench 1589 ; Serjeant 1594 ; Queen's Serjeant May 1602.

[4] Genesis xlix. 14, 15.

[5] 1603.

and nobilitie nere London : wher was declared to them that sithence the first feare by her maiestie's indisposition, the Lords hath ordered the navie to be in redines against foren attempts & divers partes of the kingdome had admonicion : so had the shiriefs lieutenants & deputie lieutenants Justices of peace throughout the kingdom : the lieutenant of the Tower the presidents of provinces & the Deputy of Ireland the maior of London, especiallie, & other corporacions : & stay made of all shippinge : therby they supposed a good securitie to the kingdome for tyme present : yet forasmuch as if god should call her maiestie, at which time the authoritie of the councellors of estate did actuallie cease, & then the nobilitie of the kingdome & such as had contynuyng authorities as corporacions by charter of inheritances & constables by common lawe, & all subiects, obliged by dutie to preserve the peace for the future successor : therfore the councell had desired the nobles to be in redines to withstand all attempt against the peace of the kingdome, wherof they were principall pillors, & to ioyne with them for some course to establish the peace in future tyme ; & said the lords were the universal & grand councell of the realme if god called her maiestie, altho during her brethinge the ordering of the peace belonged to the direcion of her privie councell : wherupon they concluded of some unitie amongest themselves : but yet I could not understand that any publick nominacion was of any certen successor, altho all spake generallie for our gracious king to ther frends privatelie : yet it semed the succession was amongest the lords & councell so assured to them, that before the Queen's deathe a proclamation was drawen redie for the signature of the lords ; and it pleased God to geve such tyme of preparacion & expectacion of her deathe, that she dying the Thursdaie after midnight, at 9 of the clocke in the morn, the councell & lords had assembled them selves at Whitehall (coming from Richmond) & ther the 24 of *March* within 8 honres after the Queen's death subscribed the Proclamation with 30 hands at least : & then instanter proclaimed the Queen's death, & the true and rightfull succession of King James the first king of England, of Scotland James the sixte. Wherupon the people both in citie & counties fynding the inst feare of 40 yeres, for want of a known successor, dissolved in a minute did so reioyce, as few wished the gracious Queue alive againe : but as the world is were inclined to alteracion of government, bothe papistes and protestants, as it semed : manie having discontentment in ther private opinions tho perhaps non in truthe : & more hoping to be bettered by the suceding kinge, in whose vertues & prudence ther is admirable expectacion. God for his mercy grant the wealth of England, & the flatterie of the Courte do not in tyme deprave his government : nor that the envie of malignant princes seek not to seduce us nor non of his subiects from ther constant obedience, nor our synnes provoke God to bereave us of so happie a kinge, untill his church be firmelie buylt & his people contynewed manie ages in the former unspeakable and admirable peace under Elizabeth.

Kinge James having by post, sent from the Lords and Councell, receved advertizement of the Queen's death, sent back, in post, a letter wherein he required the lords and councell to kepe ther attendance & assemblie still at Whitehall for preservacion of the peace : & that he purposed to contynew every officer in his place & immediatelie after sent the Lord of Kinlosse (after made master of Rolles) to shew the lords his mynd in all thinges ; but rather to be an intelligencer & an observer of all thinges, being a civilian & verie wise. About this tyme the great men sent eche secretlie ther frendes & agents into Scotland, to prepare ther way with his Maiestie, advancing ther credit, by furthering the proclamation, or because they had ben favorers of his title before, or for that they had ben with the king in the Queen's tyme : or had endured troble for desiring in parliament proclamation of his true title of succession : manie other labored ther frends to go seek places of the king before he departed Scotland, especiallie to be of his privie chamber. These all had hopefull answares.

And about the 8 of *Aprill* 1603 : the King[1] came into Barwicke, wher he was receved with great ioy as kinge : & all his way to London entertayned, with great solempnitie & state : all men reioycing that his lott & ther lott had fallen in so good a ground.[2] He was mett with great troupes of horse & wayted on

[1] James set out from Edinburgh on April 5 (Gard. *Hist.* i. p. 87).

[2] Roger Wilbraham did not neglect his own interests, as is shown by a letter from Mr. Simon Thelwal to Dr. Dunn, Dean of the Arches, and one of the Masters of Requests, then at Bremen in the Embassy mentioned above. 'Mr. Dr. Caesar and Mr. Wilbraham had, by the appointment of the Lords, set down a day to take their journey towards the King's Majesty. But Mr. Wilbraham has, it seemeth, fearing to lose his place, took post-horses, and went the day before the appoint-

by the sherief & gents of ech shire, in ther limitts : ioyfullie
receved in every citie & towne : presented with orations & guiftes
entertayned royallie all the way by noble men & gentlemen at
ther howses : & lastlie mett 4 miles from London[1] by the lord
maior & such unspeakable nomber of citizens, as the like.nomber
was never seene to issue out upon any cause before : 4 nights he
lodged at Charter Howse : four nightes more he lodged at the
Tower : during which tyme he secretlie in his coach & by water
went to see London, the Whitehall & the iewels ther (which
were said to be worth 2 millions : for that the late Queene was a
gatherer all her life, & either of nature fearefull to want in her
age, as the wisest thought, or els of providence desirous to leave
her crowne rich for the benefit of the successor & ease of her
people's charge : whose dutie is to beare the charge to support the
crowne from declination).   In every countie it pleased his maiestie
to knight the chief gents in every shire commended to him by the
nobles and favorites about him : & manie extravagants of other
counties, & some unworthy in ther proper counties, labored with
such instance to be knighted that it cam to be a great gaine (as
was thought) to the favorites.   In his maiestie's passage to his
owne howse ther were 300 knightes at the lest made, never
knowen but by report to his maiestie : & it grew a publick spech
that Englishe had the blowes & Scottish the crownes : but as it
semed the king misliking out of his royall harte that either the
unworthy should receve his favors in dignitie or that the worthy
should come to favor by unworthy meanes, removed from the
Tower to Grenewich, & ther published that such as expected
knighthood should attend till the coronation : whereby the thronge
at Courte (that evermore swarmed about his maiestie at every
back gate & privie dore, to his great offence) was sodenlie abated,
partlie by delay of ther expectacion, & because it was litle to ther
ease to attend the Court upon tber owne charges : so as his
maiestie to his iust contentment had convenient tyme to see his
howses castells forests & chases within 20 miles of London : &
therein took high delight, especiallie to see such stoare of deare
& game in his parkes for hunting, which is the sport he preferreth
above all worldlie delightes & pastime.

ment : and he did send Mr. Dr. Caesar word thereof two hours after he went out
of the town.'   (Wright's *Queen Elizabeth and her Times*, vol. ii. p. 495.
   [1] On May 3 James arrived at Theobalds (Gard. *Hist.* i. p. 100).

It is the manner, after the death of a long rayning prince, that by discontented mynds or witts starved for want of employment, manie new proiectes, sutes, invencions & infinite complaintes are brought to the successor instantlie, hoping, if they prevent discoverie, to prevaile in ther enterprises: so it happened at this tyme: for the Scottishe knowing & the Englishe coniecturing a facilitie in obtayning sutes by reason of his maiestie's most benigne & bountifull disposicion especiall towards his old servants, they never ceased to devise & sollicite sutes to his maiestie & complaints of all natures: such as were beggars were left to the ordinarie Maisters of Requests: sutes of bountie or grace were preferred by most of his Chamber, wherein the King hath ben abused by false informacions, sometymes of the qualitie of such as sued for offices, other tymes by supresing the worth of the sutes: that if his wisdome had not apeared in the cloudes, & that some wise councellors had in part fortold him, no doubt, as some escapes must ever happen in the entrance into a new government, so in these sutes for lands, pencions, offices in possession & in revercion, manie more errors had been committed to the damage of the crowne & government, & the grief of the best affected subiects.

This being a book of observations for my age or children: I writ this short & rude memoriall of the Queen's defection & the King's initiacion, as a thing most memorable wherein I note.

First: the mortalitie of princes, to make me more assured of the brevitie & incertentie of my owne lief.

Second: that when we think death furthest of, then as a thief he surprised us: for the Quene even to my self at my last audience not 5 daies before she beganne to sicken, at lest in mynd, did in extreme cold wether shew me her sommer like garments, contemning furres to withstand winter cold: & even then was death redie to knock at her dore, when nether her self her successor nor people dreamed of any such accident.

Thirdlie, I make use by the example ot David's saying that the harts of princes are in the handes of the Lord:[1] for her Maiestie (as all princes do imitating ther god) did desire perpetuall glorie above all thinges: and amongest her manifold & rare vertues of nature & arte, this was the onlie detraction that she had not power

[1] 'The king's heart is in the hand of the Lord, as the rivers of water: he turneth it whithersoever he will.' Proverbs, xxi. 1 (A.V.). 'David' must be a slip for Solomon.

to geve, wher it was merited: but was as a bailie to preserve that which she needed not in her sole person for her successor's availe: to whom God hath & will geve manie high spreading branches, that will easelie draw up the full sappe from this roote, which the former sole branche had not power to doe: & if she had disposed 20^{tie} or 30,000*l.* to the comfort of her long worne thredbare pore old servants & paid her debts, she had died, as she did, the mirrhor of her sex: so had she ben glorified by fame & love above all her best deserving progenitors: & altho that ne doubt was the highest obiect of that renowned Quene, yet she aymed amisse by his providence who wold have her (as apered in her long lyngering & willing sicknes) ioy in no worldlie thinge, but suffred her entierlie to leave them to those, of whom she was at lest ielouse, and to draw her in her end to depend upon the suer ancorhold Jesus Christ, with whom her sowle resteth.

Lastlie we & all future ages have cause to honour & admire the great providence of God that hath geven one language, one religion, one continent, & in most thinges one conformitie of lawes & customes, to thentent to unite the kingdomes, that by hostilitie of warre, were alwaies utter enemies: so as therby his church being strengthened & we, by assurance of god's eternall providence, delivered of the feare which hath perturbed the wisest of both the nations these 50 yeres, may sing *magnificat,* &c.

To conclude: because future ages will perhaps write either incertenly or variablie of our late Queue or her next successor, being both princes of highest renowne for all externall happines that nature arte or fortune can afford: I having been Master of Requests in ordinarie 3 yeres to the Queen, & 3 monethes to the Kinge, will acording to the meanes of my apprehencion without flatterie sett downe the nature & vertues with the aparant defectes in both the princes.

The Quene was of comelie personage, sound in helth till her last sicknes, strong of constitucion: her onlie phisicion was her owne observacion & good diett: not tyed to howres of eating or sleping, but following appitite: not delighted in bellie cheare to please the tast, but feding alwaies upon meates that susteyne & strenghthen nature.   In all thes habitudes the King's maiestie, her kindesman, hath semblable disposicion respecting his age & difference of sex.

The King hath a magnanimous spirite, venturous to hazard his

owne bodie in hunting especiallie & most patient of labour cold &
heate. So was the Queen farre above all other of her sex & yeres.

Both of them most mercifull in disposition : & they sone angry,
yet without bitternes or stinging revenge.

In prudence iustice & temperance, they are both the admiracion
to princes in ther severall sexes.

The King most bountifull, seldome denying any sute : the
Quene strict in geving, which age & her sex inclyned her unto :
the one often complayned of for sparinge : th'other so benigne, that
his people feare his over redines in gevinge.

The Quene slow to resolucion, & seldome to be retracted : his
maiestie quick in concluding & more variable in subsistinge.

The Queen solemne and ceremonious, & requiring decent &
disparent order to be kept convenient in ech degree : & tho she
bare a greater maiestie, yet wold she labour to entertayne strangers
sutors & her people, with more courtlie courtesie & favorable
speches then the King useth : who altho he be indeede of a more
true benignitie & ingenuous nature, yet the neglect of those
ordinarie ceremonies, which his variable & quick witt cannot
attend, makes common people iudge otherwise of him.

The Quene & King most desirous ever to please the people, &
prevent charge to them : but the Queen greved the people in
privilidges & monopolies, which I know was farre contrarie to her
princelie nature : withal mishswacion that they were profitable for
the common weal & that some of them yelded her a rent & saved
her revenew, which otherwise should have ben weakened by such
instant sutors, were the cause she graunted them : now the King
by pulling them downe & losing the profit of those rents hath pur-
chased, tho at a deare price, a sure inheritance in the love of his
people.

The Queen took delight & made profitt in simulacion & dis-
simulacion & therby discovered fashions & pretences & favorers to
sutes, & the true meaning of her severall councellors in matters of
importance : the King semes to neglecte that as bazenes, thinking
his owne witt sufficient to exploit thinges pertinent by ordinarie
meanes, without such labor & insinuacion.

The Queen was quick of apprehencion, wise in councell by
reason of her great reading & overreaching experience : of an
admirable felicitie of memorie : & albeit of great constancie, yet by
continuall labor, her benigne nature was changed & in parte

depraved by yeares & ielosies & ill affected about her : which she could hardlie eschue, being in age as a recluse cloistered to heare onlie such tunes as her kepers sounded unto her, whereby some thinges (tho good) were effected by arte of concurring in one tune that reason could never perswade her unto.

The King is of sharpest witt & invencion, redie & pithie speche, an exceding good memorie : of the swetest pleasantest & best nature that ever I knowe : desiring nor affecting any thing but true honor. As his lerning and religious vertues hath extolled him above all princes in the world, so I praie unfainedlie that his most gracious disposition & heroick myud be not depraved with ill councell, & that nether the welth & peace of England mak him forgett God, nor the painted flatterie of the Court cause him forgett himself.

At my audience 19 *July* 1603 : [1] my lord Cecill [2] secretary brought in bills to be signed by his maiesty of 8 barons & 2 erles : the earles have usuallie creacion money of £20 per annum *pro meliore sustentatione dignitatis*, but barons have none, saving the lord Mountioy hath 20 markes creacion money.

The King signed them all at one tyme confusedlie, not respecting who should have antiquitie : *quaere inde.*

The barons names were : Sir Thomas Egerton [3] lord keper, Sir William Russell [4] late lord deputie of Ireland, Sir Henry Gray [5] lieutenant of the gard, Sir John Harington, [6] Sir John Peter, [7] Sir Henry Danvers, [8] Sir Thomas Gerard [9] knight marshall, Sir Robert Spencer. [10]

The lord Thomas Howard made erle of Suffolk : & the lord Mountioy, lord lieutenant of Ireland, made erle of Devonshire.

---

[1] The King was at *H*ampton Co*u*rt. Nichols's *Progresses of James I.*, i. 204.

[2] Cecil had been raised to the *P*eerage by the title of Baron Cecil of Essendon on May 13, 1603.

[3] Baron Ellesmere.

[4] Yo*u*nger son of Francis, second Earl of Bedford, created Baron R*u*ssell of Thornha*u*gh.

[5] Baron Grey of Groby.   Baron *H*arington of Exton.

[7] Baron Petre of Writtle.

[8] Baron Danvers of Dantesy ; afterwards Earl of Danby.

[9] Baron Gerard of Gerard's Bromley.

[10] Baron Spencer of Wormleighton.

This day also the lord keper brought in a newe great seale : & had the old defaced & cutt in peces by the king himself & in his sight in presence of most of the councell called therto into the privie chamber : after which the king made an actuall delivery of the new seale to the lord keper *de novo* : & allowed him the old seale as a perquisite : of which a entry is in chauncery for memoriall therof.

21 *Julii*: erle de Southampton[1] dudum attaint ad novel creacion de son erledome : et lez avant ditz 2 erles & 8 barons fueront solempment par lection de lour lettres patentz a eux et al beires males de lour corps : et par endument de hood sur lour robes par le roy meme : et par cap de maintenance.[2]

25 *July* St James his day : was King James crowned first king of England & Ireland of that name & 6 king of Scotland : it was at Westminster : when ther died of the plague 1500 a weeke in London, the suburbes and tounes next adioining : & a proclamation to restraine accesse of people, & the feast usuall at coronation forborne, the King & Queen coming from Whitehall to Westminster private, made the nomber of people and the pompe much lesse.

Yet the presence of the nobilitie, bishops, officers about the king's person, 60 knightes of the Bath then made : the presence of the iudges & serieants, singing men, trumpeters & musicions, made a great assemblie ; besides manie ambassadors from divers countreyes. At the Coronation when the King & Queen had seated themselves on ther throane of estate, erected nere the alter & spred with cloth of silver & gold : Garter Harold proclaimed in ech 4 angles and quarters in the King's hearing, demanding of the people whether they wold have King James ther king : in ech place with applaude, showting, throwing up hatz they assented.

Then the King had praiers said before his chaire, and the crowne put on by the Archbishop of Canterberi[3] and Deane of

---

[1] Henry Wriothesly, attainted and imprisoned in 1598.

[2] This entry in the MS. comes between the discussion in the Council on the Irish coin and the report of the dissolution of the Parliament of 1603, but at the top of a blank page, entirely apart from them. As the date of this recreation is given in *S. P. Dom.* 1603–10, p. 23, I have altered the order of the entry.

[3] John Whitgift.

Westminster [1] with praiers, and had auncient robes that were
Edward the Confessor's put on & took oathes, due to the King;
hard a sermon preched by the bishop of Winchester: [2] was
anoynted head shoulders & sides standing in his dublett cutt open
for that purpose & receved the communion: and after removing
from the altar to the throne & theater, receved homage of all the
English nobilitie; and then the Lord keper published to the
people, in the 4 severall quarters of the theater 4 severall tymes,
that the King had granted to his people a most ample & generall
pardon as ever prince did: at the which the people againe with
showtes praied for the King: and so the King retorned to the
Whitehall privatelie: the Queen also was then crowned & anoynted
Queen: the eternall god blesse them & ther royall posteritie: &
make them, as heades, & ther subiects, one firme solide & perpetuall bodie.

6 *Aug.* 1603: 4 Agents from the nobilitie & gentry of Ireland
were committed to the Tower, for presenting a peticion to have
the publick use of ther religion, & to be governed with ther owne
nacion: & they have ther coyne better,[3] the religion could not be
altered but by parliament, & ther action herein tended to sedition: also the peticion was presented by them having assembled
30 or more persons of the nobles & gentlemen of Ireland that
attended for other sortes, as tho the wold put his maiestie in feare,
if he graunted not ther uniust desire.

They were told at the commitment that his maiestie was firm
in his faithe; & some said he said in some publik audience, he
wold rather fight in bloud to the knees then geve tolleracion of
religion.

7 *Aug.*: The Lords finding the Queen's funerall, the King's
coronation, his attendance to be brought in, his liberall giftes &
such extraordinarie charges, had spent the treasure, sent to
Londoners to borow £40,000 who answered faintlie:

These 4 proposicions were made to encrease the King's treasure: proponed by the Lord Treasurer.

---

[1] Lancelot Andrewes.   [2] Thomas Bilson.
[3] It was not till the autumn of 1604 that the disastrous policy of a debased
coinage was finally abandoned in Ireland (Gard. *Hist.* i. 373).

1° to sell all copiholders ther frehoulds, which was thought the rediest way:

2° to grant leases for 60 yeres of all the kinge's lands, or fee farmes, taking small fines and dobling or trebling the rents ·

3° to have composicion for respite of homage :

4° the Master of Wardes [1] said he was to have wardes torned to a certain annual rent to be propounded in parliament.

Monday 9 *Sept.* : 1603 : I was at Oxford ; wher lying at the Crosse Inne, the best in the citie, yet was ther two howses on either side adioyning infected with plague : [2] *sed deus nos protegat.*

There was the Spanishe Ambassador lodged in Christchurch and the Archduke's Ambassador lodged in Mawdelin Colledge : the attended ther audience at the king's coming to Wodstock.[3]

I surveyed the chiefest colledges : 1° Christchurch which was ment to have ben a famous monument, but never finished by the founder Cardinall Wolsey : it was ment to be a square of 8 score three parts built, but the churche not builded : ther is the fairest hall with great church windoes, & the largest kichin I ever sawe.

Mawdelins is the second chief colledge : a large uniform square, about 4 score yardes within & all clostered benethe : a hall with church windoes, & a chappell fairer then faire & lardge churches : ther are walkes sufficient to environ a litle towne : for besides a close of x acres walled about for walkes & severall divided walks with ash trees, they have manie orchards walled in, & ech chamber to 2 Fellows have a peculiar orcharde.

---

[1] Cecil succeeding his father.

[2] Anthony Wood gives a vivid description of this plague visitation. Michael- mas Term could not be kept, and all the gates of the colleges and balls were con- stantly kept shut day and night, and only a few persons left in them to keep pos- session (*Hist. and Antiq. of the Univ. of Oxford* [1796], ii. 280).

[3] The Spanish Ambassador, Don Juan de Taxis, Count of Villa Mediana, and the Count of Aremberg, the Archduke's Ambassador, had lately arrived in England to negotiate a peace. (Gard. *Hist.* i. 117, 207.) Sir Thomas Edmonds, in a letter to the Earl of Shrewsbury, dated September 11, 1603, Woodstock, writes: ' By reason that the Spanishe Ambassador hath had one of his company lately dead of the Plague at Oxford, his audience, which was appointed to have been given him here, is deferred till the King's coming to Winchester.' (Nichols's *Progresses,* i. 258-9.)

They have walkes also made in the medowes wherin the
river of Temmies, & of Charwell do runne & meete; invironed
close walk of willow & some elmes, to walk the distance of
half a mile, in shadowes : this is the most compleet & fairest
colledg & walks in England : (tho Trinitie Colledg square is much
larger & fairer.)

Martyn College is a second to this & with statlie hall &
chappell & square equall almost to Mawdelin : & I think a cloister
in a second court fairer : a faire garden but not such large walks
as the former.

All Sowles Colledg doth almost equall Martyn Colledg, but the
square not so great : & without cloister.

Brazen Nose Colledg hath a nose of brass upon the gate : it is
a pretie square uniform, but the hall square & chappell nothing to
the former : yet statelie & colledg like : & to this most colledgs
in Cambridg are equall.

Universitie Colledg is the auncientest Colledg : Jesus Colledg,
Lincolne Colledg & others I saw on the outside : they seme farr
inferior to the former.

All these 4 great colledgs have ther halles mounted 20 steppes
from above the ground : but in Cambridge the halls stand upon
the grounde : & all in Oxford built of free hewen stone : the most
in Cambridg of bricke.

Yet the gatehouses & coming into Trinitie & St Johns in
Cambridge is more statelie then any in Oxford.

Ther is 16 Colledges & 8 Halles in Oxford.

Eche of the 5 colledges I surveyed have good libraries ; but
the chiefest wonder in Oxford is a faire Divinitie Schole with
church windoes : and over it the fairest librarie called the
Universitie Librarie founded & supplied dailie by Mr. Bodley,
that is thought for bewtie of building & wainscott frames &
chaynes to kepe the books, will equall any in christendome : all
the windoes of all the libraries have but two lightes & a transome,
& sett nere together of equall distance, the one half wall thother
windowe, by equall distance.[1]   All the Colledg windowes are

---

[1] The year before, 1602, had seen the achievement of Sir Thomas Bodley's
offer, made to the Vice-Chancellor in 1598, to restore Duke Humphrey's library
'to it's former use and to make it fit and handsome with scates and shelves and
deskes and all that may be needful to stir up other men's benevolence to help to

likewise but 2 lightes, & some have transomes & some none · & the toppe of ech window is not flatt or square, but round as an arch at the toppe.

Mawdelins, Martyn Colledg & as I remember All Sowles Colledges wer builded by 3 successive bishops of Winchester [1] wholie : the towne of Oxford fairer & larger then Cambridge, but Cambridge hath a farre fairer markett place.

Oxford stands lowe, with rich meadowes about the rivers that runne by it : & Oxford is invironed with pretie litle hills two miles off by south & west : that part northward a flatt : the soile is clay & sand : a lighter ground & mold.

But Cambridge standes in a large flatt every way close to the river : & in a miry depe clay soile : all arable about it, in effect wanting the pleasure of medowes.

This progresse, *Sept* : 1603, I saw Salisberie called New Salisberie : th'old stoad on the toppe of a hill, & decayed for want of water.

Wherupon the towne was about E. 3 tyme builded two miles off in a flatt low ground & builded upon piles : the towne is built chequerwise, that at ech center you may look into 4 streetes : & ther is a river whereby ther be drawen into every streete a streme of water contynuallie runninge.

Ther is a rare faire & large cathedrell church in this citie, built by the bishop ther : & the building contynewed 40 yeres : & the charges aperes by the old books.

The Earle of Pembroke hath 2 miles off a faire howse called Wilton,[2] a large & high built square of hewen stone : the roames having ther lightes but one way into the square are malencholik & dark.

furnish it with books (Anthony Wood, *Hist., &c., of the University of Oxford* [1796], ii. pp. 265-6). Casaubon, who visited Oxford in 1613, writes of the Bodleian as 'a work rather for a king than a private man.' The divinity school both for its architecture and the library contained in it has his unstinted praise. 'Nothing in Europe is comparable.' (Boase's *Oxford*, p. 139.)

[1] There is some error here : only Waynflete, the founder of Magdalene, was a Bishop of Winchester.

[2] The seat of William Herbert, Earl of Pembroke, where James I. passed part of September 1603 and the whole of October (Nichols's *Progresses of James I.* i. 281).

Two miles from Salisberie on th'other side, Sir Thomas Gorge hath built a faire new howse [1] of stone, a triangle with 3 great round towers at ech end, wherein are his fairest chambers: & he hath the fairest garden & grene walks invironed with the river, & grenesward court before his gate, that I have seene: all his windowes are but 2 lightes with a transome, & yet being sett thick & uniform shew well & faire: but hath few lodging in his howse: it is much spent in pantreyes.

The first *Christmas* of worthy king James was at his court at Hampton, A° 1603: wher the French,[2] Spanish [3] & Polonian Ambassadors were severallie solemplie feasted: manie plaies & daunces with swordes: one mask by English & Scottish lords: another by the Queen's Maiestie & eleven more ladies of her chamber presenting giftes as goddesses.[4]   These maskes, especialli the laste, costes 2000 or 3000[l], the aparells: rare musick, fine songes: & in iewels most riche 20000[l], the lest to my´iudgment: & her maiestie 100000[l]: [5] after Christmas was running at Ring by the King & 8 or 9 lords for the honour of those goddesses & then they all feasted together privatelie.

Jan. 1603.   The King's maiestie had an assemblie of the church bishops, & of the lernedst devines called puritans: and after 3 daies conference whereat I was witness the devines confessed scruples: corner cap: crossing in baptism: rings in marriage. Homelies read in churches wher wante lerned prechers, kneling at communion, common praier with preching, confirmacion of children, private baptisme so it were by a minister, to be verie auncient in the primitive church: & the two last to be necessarie, thother indifferent, & to be admitted for decency & unitie: & the king's maiestie will have some things in the book of common praier explained to take away scandall: the herizies in the Apocripha not to be reade: & all the church brought to this unitie by moderacion, & perswacion of bishops to prechers that be honest & not contencious: but seismatical prechers to be coerced ·

---

[1] Longford Castle.   [2] Beaumont.   [3] Villa Mediana.

[4] This masque, by Daniel, is in Nichols's *Progresses*, i. 305–311*, and was played on January 8, 1604 n.s.

[5] During the first four years of the reign 92,000*l*. were spent in jewels alone (*Parliamentary Debates*, 1610.   Camden Society, vol. 81, Introduction, p. xv).

allowance geven to the 3 articles they are to subscribe, being reade, as I remember were :

1. The King's supremacie allowed by all, as governour : spirituall men to do ther duties in ther callings.

2. Nothing in the common praier book, these obscurities explaned, dissonant from the word of God.

3. The articles ratified by parliament not to be contrariant to the canonicall scripture.

It is resolved a new translation shalbe of the bible : and this common catichism with some enlargement to be in every church said, not divers nor long cathechisms : for discipline, the rigour & abuse of excomunicacion, the iudges & bishops to devise another censure : for planting a lerned ministerie, in the north, Wales & Ireland, commissioners apointed : to reforme *quantum potest*. The King's Maiestie concluded an unitie in indifferent things : but in matter essenciall to salvacion, better to obey God then man. Predestinacion & elecion not meeto to be preched, but with great respect, & that as a father said to be believed *adscendendo*, begyning at our sanctificacion, which doth argue iustificacion : & that argues calling and elecion : & that ther is an inseparable linke & coniunction of these 4 : & the frailtie such as non can be presumptuouslie assured of his elecion, but must work his salvacion with feare, & out of workes to prove his calling : *Rex doctissimus et eloquentissimus disputator omnium : idque coram clero.*

The Commissioners for the Hanse Townes in Germanie have had often conference with the Lords, 23 *Sept.* 1604.

They claime auncient privilidges in England, granted by E. 2 : & after confirmed by patent & parliament by E. 4.

Ther chief clayme is to be as free of all customes as English borne for all transportacions & importacion & to be free of all trades & in all tounes in England.

This contynued till E. 6 made an order by his councell, *A*° 6°, proving those liberties forfett : first because they were no corporacion capable therof; but chiefli by abusing the liberties in coloring foreners goods, denying us lik mutuall commerce with them, enlarging ther *Hanses* and ther trade to the ruyno of Englishe. Queen Marie, at the instance of King Philip, condiscended to some liberties : but the *Hanses* never accepted therof, but have made ever challenges to them : & having some moderacions of those liberties ofred them by Queen Elizabeth, the refused, and caused the Emperor by strict mandate to inhibite us the Empyre, *circa* 89 : (the Staade and other cities have entertayned our merchants for the necessitie they have of our wolls & clothes).

And now after deliberacon & by his Maiestie's direcion the *Hanses* have ther answare this 23 *Sept.* 1604 at Hampton Court.[1]

First that the king & councell find ther auncient liberties void *causa predicta* : & the same denied these last 60 yeres to them : Touching ther desire to have some new treatie for more moderate liberties, *utrimque*; answare was, that the state of England might not endure them to be as free as English in customes especiallie : for so our trade of our merchants wold be overthrowen, & our navie decay : but they were offred to have as great liberties as any foren in amitie with the king have : & to grant them more, were to draw on the king the dailie importunitie and mislike of other princes.

Note the mischief to allow them equall fredom with Englishe in custom (which is doble custom to strangers) is that the *Hanses* carying in bottomes farre cheper, & having more alliance & fredome in passing the Sound & otherwise then English, they might sell better chepe, & ingrose our clothes & stoppe & open our vent & trade at ther wills : and therfore the *Hanses* being denyed ther liberties with protestacions of all other amitie, as to have ther *stilliard* howse or such lik curtesie, departed, not expecting so finall an answare.

All our feare is, if the *Hanses* have creditt with the Emperour, he will proclaime a new inhibicion against us : but our merchants answare the *Hanses* have no such interest in the Emperour, & manie tounes in the confines of the Empire & Denmark will desire the residence of our trade staple, so precious as they cannot want it.

It semes by often debates of Councellours, that it is unmeete by concluding peace [2] with Spain we should geve him the redier passage to command Holland & the Low Countreys : for therby

---

[1] The Order in Council rejecting the claim of the *H*anse Towns to certain ancient privileges as injurious to trade is dated Sept. 30, 1604, *H*ampton Court (*S. P. Dom.* i. 1603–10, p. 154).

[2] The treaty of peace with Spain was sworn to by James on August 19, 1604 (Gard. *Hist.* i. 214). It was not until 1609 that the Dutch, by the truce signed at Antwerp, obtained from Spain a recognition of their independence.

we should have to stronge a neighbour to nere us, as Spaine is : which were to bring us to perill dailie if he fall in his faith & peace : & if the articles of peace be broken in small matters, it is not like the king will warre against any of them, especiallie for wrongs to merchandize, &c., being private, but live in amitie with both.

12 *Jan.* 1604. Al hunting al Roiston : [1] Roy et deane de chapell [2] cite 12 deutronomy [3] : sur que ascun seer que chescun poet expend son dismes de meme : et deane dit que sont 3 kindes de dismes, destre view in ceo chapter : 1° Aniversariae decimae, solubiles tantum presbiteris : 2° Triennarie solubiles presbiteris ut Dei gloria elargietur pauperibus : 3° Festivales decimae, ou al festivals iours chescun carier ou eschaunger ses dismes, et al esglise ferra fest par luy son familie & ses filz & files, in gloria Dei : issint chescun an deux dix partes serra expend al esglise et glorie de dieu : et chescun 3 an serra 3 tres dismes pay ut supra.

Et Roy dit que auncient testament est plus direct pur dismes que novel : et ils ne remember ascun lieu pur enforcer personall dismes, comme lez dix partes de gaines de merchants ou legis peritorum, &c.

18 *Jan.* 1604, Mr Harley my host at Huntingdon told me this night, supping with me, that he being before a farmer & 24 horses for plows 12 horses & xxx cattall were bewitched & died in ii daies, soddainlie sick, crying & grynnyng & staringe : in th'end was advised to burne a sick horse alive & so did, and after had no more died : another did so by his shepo by Harley's advise : non after died : & Harley said a knowen witch advised him to burne the hart by rosting on a spitt, & the witch wold come to the dore before the hart was rosted.

The king's maiestie, sithence his happie comyng, by his owne

---

[1] ' The King went to Royston two days after Twelfth-tide, where and thereabouts he hath continued ever since, and finds such felicity in that hunting life that he hath written to the Council that it is the only means to maintain his health (Chamberlain to Winwood, Jan. 26. Winwood's *Memorials*, ii. 46).

[2] James Montague, Dean of Worcester, 1604; Bishop of Bath and Wells, 1608, and of Winchester, 1616 ; edited the collected edition of the King's works brought out in 1616 (*Dic. Nat. Bio.*).

[3] 12 *Deuteronomy*, on Tithes.

skill hath discovered 2 notorious impostures : one of a phisicion that made latyne & lerned sermons in the slepe : which he did by secret premeditacion : thother of a woman pretended to be bewitched, that cast up at her mouth pynnes, & pynnes were taken by divers in her fitts out of her brest.

The last Sunday in *October* 1605, Sir Georg Carew,[1] Treasurer of Ireland, made peticion to have his great acompt finished by the Lords Commissioners : Answare was made that Sir John Ramsay[2] had begged of his Maiestie the benifite of the deceates in the Tresorer's acompts & that his maiestie willed a staie : the lord chauncellor said in H. 6[3] tyme, a generall complaint was to parliament against Michael de la Pole chauncellor, & being referred the iudges said it was to generall & not by the lawes to be answared unto : therupon the same was drawen into more particularitie & so obiected & answared in parliament : so this complaint against the Treasurer is now followed by M[r] Ramsay defending before 4 principal of the Councell.

Deo gratias.

The 5 of *Nov.* 1605 : the Lords & Commons attended to expect the King's coming the begynning of this parliament then to be held by prorogation :

A week before, the Lord Mountegle imparted to the King & Council, a letter sent to his hands by one unknowen & fled :[4]

---

[1] Sir George Carew, or Carey, Lord Deputy, for a brief space, between the terms of Mountjoy and Chichester, had left Ireland in July 1604, though his permanent recall was not until October (Gard. *Hist.* i. 373). He had held the office of Treasurer at War in Ireland (*ibid.* i. 372). Besides incurring the usual enmities and charges of rapacity Carew had offended Mountjoy by a rash speech. In March 1605 he is directed to submit the ledger book of the accounts of his Treasurership for the wars ending September 30, 1604 (*Cal. of S. P. Irel.*, 1603_6, p. 269).

[2] Sir John Ramsay had been the Ki g's page at the time of the Gowrie conspiracy, when he stabbed Ruthven. In 1606 James created him Viscount Haddington, and in 1620 Earl of Holderness. The records of the reign are full of gifts and grants to him. See *S. P. Dom.* xxvi. 45, as quoted by Gardiner, i. 330). On Oct. 25, 1605, Salisbury in a letter to Lake speaks of 'Sir John Ramsay's complaint of deceit' (*S. P. Dom.* 1603_10, p. 237).

[3] A mistake for Richard II.

[4] Monteagle received the letter at his house at Hoxton on October 26, 1605;

wherein he was advised to be absent from the parliament, for that undoutedlie, some great calamitie wold happen soddainlie by un-knowen accident, which wold be as soddaine as the fyring of the letter :[1] wherupon the king after one serch about Parliament Howse grew so ielouse he caused a secrett watch, & discovered one Johnson practizing about midnight to make a traine to fyre 3 l. barrels powder, hidden under billettz in a vault inst under the Upper Howse of Parliament,[2] confessed by one Johnson servant to Thomas Percy, a pentioner, to have ben preparing 8 moneth to blow up the King, his Queen, children, nobles, bishops, iudges & all the commons assembled, if it had not been so happelie dis-covered. So the parliament was proroged till this Saterdaie : in the meane tym the said Percy & Robert Catesbie Esq', who sold me Radborne pastures 5 yeres sithence, stirred an assemblie of desperate bankeroutz pretending advancement of catholik religion to the nomber of 200 in Warwickshire & Worcester : upon which occasion the parliament this day proroged till the 21 of *January* 1605, being Tuesdaie, as the day wherein the king had scaped Gow-rye's conspiracy in Scotland, & this horrible practise in England.[3] But before publishing the adiornement, the lord chancellor [4] made grave spech : of our cause of unspekable alacritie that had united bothe these imperiall crounes under the soveraintie of his royal person : & for happie establishing therof the commissioners of both lands had concluded of certen articles tripartite, under ther seales : one part delivered to his maiestie,

and took it at once to Whitehall, where he found Salisbury, Nottingham, Suffolk, Worcester, and Northampton at supper. The letter was not shown to the King until November 3.

[1] There are no such words in the letter; but the King took a pleasure in allowing it to be believed that he discovered the plot from the words 'the danger is past as soon as you have burnt the letter.' See Gard. *Hist.* i. pp. 248-50, where the letter is given. The letter also spoke of 'a terrible blow this Parliament, and yet they shall not see who hurts them.'

[2] The first search was made by Suffolk as Lord Chamberlain on November 4, at about 3 o'clock (Gard. *Hist.* i. 250). At 11 o'clock the same night was made the further search which resulted in the capture of Fawkes.

[3] November 5 fell on a Tuesday: the date of the Gowrie conspiracy was August 5, 1600.

[4] Parliament, which had reassembled on November 5, was prorogued until January 21, 1606 (Gard. *Hist.* i. 285). Of the Lord Chancellor's speech there is a bare summary contained in a few lines in the *Parliamentary History* (i. 1052).

2 parts to the chauncelor of Scotland[1] to be presented at ther parliament, the 3 part he presented to the lords & commons now sealed with all the commissioners seals, according to the act of the last parliament.

He said it was no union to abolish the names of England & Scotland: no alteracion of lawes or the points of government or pollicy; but *proiect pur perfecion de union al benefite* of both kingdomes: wherof he praied favorable construcion, of ther sincere proceding: he compared this tyme with the late tyme of our Q. Elizabeth of famous memorie, & former tymes when the cr:ueltiof civill warres was extinguished by the union of the howses of Lancaster & York: yet that union was clouded with mist & doubt even in the middest of the raigne of H. 8; but the union of the king's succession is perpetuall, by uniting in his person two kingdoms, wherein the severall monarches have had so long discents in ther blond as no king christian hath the like: & this union is the act of god, not patched by absolucions of popes or parliament to dispense with doubtfull or illegittimate mariages.

Also in the late Q[s] tyme, *senectus et orbitas* were feared in her, & induced hopes to the Pope & foreners to drawe us to foren subiection: besides the Novelestes & sectaries in religion, who wold be subiect to no commaund, made us in more daunger then when ther was a Heptarchie.

His Maiestie is of ripe yeres, longe experience in kinglie state wherin his strength hath ben tried: his wisdome, iustice, vertue & science admirable.

In lieu of orbitie, the Queen a fruitefull vine, & 4 olive branches of extraordinarie vertue & hopefull posteriti: he hath planted ecclesiasticall government: all foren princes have sued to him for peace to his honour, so are we established: & foreners, some said was not possible this establishment, find it firme & no hope for foreners: Justices in nomber increased: no officer displaced.

But what thankfulness in us, alas Winchester is witnese of the first attempt of Rawley[2] &c.: & we have sene the horrible attempte the last day against king, nobles, prelates & commons.

This procedes both first & last from romish pristes by a hellish practise under the earth.

[1] Alexander Seton, Earl of Dunfermline.

[2] Raleigh's trial was held at Winchester, November 17, 1603 (Gard. *Hist.* i. 123).

These have raized a nomber like Catelyn's camp of wasters &
spend goods to stirre rebellion, not so wise as Balam's asse, who
discerned god's army : praied the king for suero iustice *ne pars
sincera trahatur* : the papistes may be Christians but corrupt
romish Christians.

Millions have geven ther hartes to the king to ayde him with
ther goods & lands & sacrifice ther lives for his service ·

He praieth exemplarie punishment in these may cause others to
abhorre romishe religion : & praieth Christ Jesus to preserve his
maiestie & progenie for ever.

The king's speech : [1] ' I had occasion the last parliament to
render thankfulnes for the loyaltie of your hartes upon my coming ·
now I am to render to god thanks for our safe delivery, *misericordia
domini super omnia opera eius.*

The creacion of man not so glorious as his redempcion, the old
Adam not so glorious as the new : so this delivery greter then our
accesse to the crown ; *vox faucibus haeret.*

The daunger so gret, the cause so litle : in that place they
thought to reveng hard lawes : in that we are to magnifie our god.
God geves sparkes & attributes of divinitie to king that rules litle
world under him.

The great world he destroes by water, the deluge, & fire, to
purge the godlie, destroy the wicked. So the hiest places subiect
to most daunger : which he had tasted first by Rawlie's
conspiracie, wher he should have ben bathed in bloud :
sed inciderunt in foveam quam fecerunt : so this last by fire, a
daunger from a senseless element more inevitable then any of men,
or bestes which Daniel escaped.

It was miraculouse being attempted by subiects without cause,
pretending religion & conscience : & no remorse therof either in
the prisoners or the rebells abroad.

Miracle to have a king distroyed in parliament *inter* nobles &
commons *pur consult de bone publik*, the proper place & function of

---

[1] There are two full reports of the King's speech, (1) Lords' *Journals*, ii.
357-9 ; (2) *Parliamentary History*, 1054-1062, whereof the second is the fuller.
Roger Wilbraham's report, though condensed, gives the general sense ; yet, while
omitting no material point, it differs somewhat in the words used. Thus
Raleigh is not mentioned in the Lords' *Journals* or *Parliamentary History* by
name.

a king: they confesse the chose this enterprise as *minus malum* to destroy all then the king to escape.

A miracle the king, taxed with want of suspicion in confidence of his owne sinceritie, should, against advise of councell, be extraudinarie suspicious: & collect the daunger out of the words of the letter, otherwise then devine or lawier wold interpret.

Scipio accused for wasting treasure, answared & was clered by saying, ' this day I wanne a victorie,' so in this place I may use divinitie in geving thanks for deliverie in this place:

I wishe my hart were sene in a glasse: this act hath not moved me to crueltie nor to ielosie of anie, but shall geve me caution to distinguish daungers & men.

These malefactors were prophane & bankroutz endevoring the distrocion of the state.

I have not read of Turkish or Jewish religion *que ad maintene* murder of the king & people: yet here religion is made the cause: & so are the Jesuits as allies, & others of this wicked mind.'

He distinguished of papistes: such as hold those doctrines be no good subiects: other be, & may be saved, tho they beleve 7 sacraments & such-like if at ther death they assure themselves in Jesus: & he warned those half papist, to detest alters & such: & said he wold proroge this parliament for the service against these rebels, who by repaire of all men of sort to the parliament have stood out hitherto; & for whose confusion he wished every one might endevor the uttermost, & that these rebels might be declared in parliament for a perpetual memorie of ther detestacion having offended the parliament universal.

Against the next session, wher he is no bound to be present, he advised the howse to remember, parliaments are consultacions of the king as heade: & his nobles are hereditarie parliament: & commons elective parliament *pro tempore* & the assemblie apointed to propone causes for the general profitt touching peace or warre: & no private bills, purporting generall, but ayming the good of some particuler for opression.

Lacedimonians allowed non to propound a new lawe, but with a rope about his neck.

Lett no puritane or malignant propone or utter affectionate speches: avoid rethorik & propound ech thing with sinceritie & gravitie.

He protested he wold propone nothing in parliament unlesse

ıt tended to the equall good of both kingdoms, loving them equallie.

Lett all things be so caried with wisdome as no parti depart discontent, king nor people : but let ther be a wise & loving coniunction for the weale publik against the conspirators therof.

And so the lord chauncelor was commanded to pronounce the adprorogacion of parliament.

In the cession of parliament 3 *Regis Jacobi*:[1] for 7 weekes nothing done for any publique bill : nor no private bill passed both howses within that tyme ; the tyme most while spent in invectives against purveiors : & concerning a bill for redresse of those enormities : & upon conferences with the lords touching an act for the king's safetie, & further punishements, restraintes & discoverie of popish recusants, wherein both howses made declamations & manie devises of proiects against them : wherein they were extraordinarie incensed by occasion of the late horible practize of gunpowder discovered, which they conceve proceded of out the religion of Jesuitisme, wherein for advauncement of the church of Rome, excommunicacion, deposicion & murder of princes is held lawfull, & either meritorious or by dispensacion before, or absolucion after to be pardoned, altho manie Romanistes pretend the facts horrible.

Touching purveiors.[2]   (After the commons had frelie offred the king 2 subsidies & 4 fiftenths :)[3]   The lords anotamized to the commons upon conference,[4] that the king had kept a long christmas : & ben at extraordinario charges : the Q^s funerall 40000[1] : the bringing in of the King, Queen & Prince 100 : giftes to Ambassadors 4000 :[5] the emptines of the Q^s cofers : increase of

---

[1] Parliament met January 21, 1606.

[2] Of the conferences and debates on the grievance of purveyance which this entry and those dated March 11 and April 15 deal with there is a somewhat confused summary in the *Parliamentary History* (i. 1065). The Commons' efforts to pass a Bill were wrecked by the resistance of the Lords (Gard. *Hist.* i. 299). See Spedding's *Letters and Life of Francis Bacon* (iii. 259, &c.), where an attempt is made to reproduce from the *Commons' Journals* the course of these conferences and debates. Wilbraham, as a member of the committee which met the Lords (*C. J.* i. 268), here gives a more coherent account.

[3] February 10.

[4] February 14 & 19. See C. *J.* i. 269 and 271.

[5] In *Commons' Journals* the accounts given differ—*i.e.* Queen's funeral,

new charges: the reliques of charges in Ireland & Berwick: charges of guiftes & pencions, for rewards, for bounti, for importunitie: wherby decay of revenewe hath groen: increase of iudges & officers in all places: the dett of the late Queen about 400000^l, increased now by these & other meanes to 774000^l: [1] the virginitie of the K^s promises for repayment of privie seales like to be lost, to his great dishonour: & finallie his state not able to subsist unlesse by composicion annuall for taking away the purveyors for ever, which were termed vulturs, harpies, cormorants & caterpillers & vermyne, some supply might be devised (for advauncing the king's declyning state) by the commons.

The commons in publik debated & most voices semed to mislike the composicion annuall·

1° it wold be a perpetuall rent charge throughout England & a burden for ever:

2° next it was supposed by the lawiers of the common howse, (tho in the face of all the iudges drawen to the conference by the Lords to clere all doubtes, who delivered no resolute opinion therein, nether were much urged thereto: & *per case* doubtful in the matter:) that the king's maiestie had by prerogative onlie a preempcion but no prerogative in price: tho the Lords said the King found the crowne possessed by long prescripcion of a prerogative to have a resonable price to all his empcions for his houshold.

To which was answered the king could not prescribe against the statutes made in point direct to the contrarie.

3° The great obiection against composicion was that the king nor parliament could not secure the composicion: (which manie think may be done especiallie for the K^s tyme, when he shall receve a annuall satisfacion *exercitorie*): for if 36 actes of parliament cannot restore the people to ther right of inheritance against purveors, one act now is not available: but as I think those acts were rather acts of restraint of abuses then acts of abolishing the name & use altogether which upon mutuall & equall consideracion may be done:

4° If it be true that the prerogative is to have purveyance in

20,000l.; bringing in of the King, &c., 10,000l.; gifts to ambassadors, 40,000l. (*C. J.* i. 271.)

[1] Gardiner gives total debt at 735,280l. (*Hist.* i. 295), basing it on the Lord Treasurer's declaration (*S. P. Dom.* xix. 45).

price also, & that inherent in the crowne : it cannot be sold nor severed : nether is it honorable :

5° Our bill against them is to restore us to our true libertie of inheritance : if this our inheritance should be against [us] bought, or if we buy our lawes of iustice, it were dishonorable to so gracious a king : & pernicious in future examples :

6° I thinke a great doubt may be that when the king's children's children shall increase his famelie, for the nephewes & all lineal discendants (*quaere de collateral freres*, &c.) are to be parcell of the kinges household in prerogative : then & upon all sugestions by suceding kinges, the composicion may be said to litle : & so to be increased upon the subiect : or els purveiors to be cast upon them for an afflicion, if they refuse to compound.

It was further moved by the commons to increase our subsidie : [1] (for 15[thes] lay upon pore tounes verie hevie [2]) reasoned that the necessitie of the king must be releved by the affectionate love of the people : the king is the hart, the head, & lief of our lawes & commonweale : & the Chauncellor of eschequer [3] said the King was like Theodosius, the good Emporour, who said, *etsi legibus soluti simus tamen secundum leges vivere volumus* : & this is cited as a rule in the civil lawe ; & so grief or want in the hart & hed must be releved by the helpe of all other members as the most obnoxious :

'Treasure is said to be the sinews of the commonweal : & the contraction of the sinewes in the brayne bredes a cramp & convulsion in all the inferior parts,' saieth Bond [4]: the benignitie, bountie, & pietie of our king & his necessitie amplified by many proverbs.

[1] On March 25 an additional subsidy and two-fifteenths were voted (*C. J.* i. 289).

[2] From the eighth year of Edward III. the assessment of the lay tenths and fifteenths took a settled form : the several districts were permanently rated at the amount paid in that year ; particular incidence being determined by the local authority. The small towns, in many instances fallen in wealth and population, would be assessed at the same amount as 250 years before (Gard. *Hist.* i. 297 ; Stubbs, *Const.* Hist. ii. 576).

[3] In *Commons' Journals* (i. 279) this speech seems to be assigned to ' Mr. Chancellor, Sir John Fortescue.' Fortescue had been Chancellor of the Exchequer until the beginning of James's reign, when he gave way to Sir George Hume ; but a new patent from the King in 1603 confirmed him in his office of Chancellor of the Duchy of Lancaster for life (*Dict. Nat. Bio.*).

[4] John Bond, M.P. for Taunton (*Parl. Hist.* i. 975).

Amplificacion for subsidie made : by foren princes greter imposicions : the king's mild usage of his unlimited prerogative : & mild taxes :

Also it is for our's more then his safetie : also this tyme, when our straiter lawes will excite the pope & his adherents to attempt hostilitie : also daungerous the king's povertie being knowen & not releved may prevoke our reconciled enemies or our malignant negbors to unusuall attempts.

9 *Marcii* : 1605, Sir Edward Clere was called before the councell for a contempt, in assuming the order of knighthood & St Michaell with a patent therof from the French king : it was first resolved the general order of knighthood might be acepted as a generall favour from any foren prince : but to take the order of St Michael, being an order wherby his dutie of allegeance to the king is in part obliged to the foren king this is most unlawfull & undutifull : especiallie if he have taken an oath, which ties him to observe some orders incident : & altho he took no othe yet he is bound to observe the institucions of the order : & therfore without the king's licence may not assume it : he was therfore committed to the Marshalsie of the king's howse, with order no man should arest him : but if he had ben committed to the Marshalsie of King's Bench or Fleete, the Lords' warrant could not have prohibited, but execucions out of those courtes of Bench & Common Plees wold have ben laid upon him, as was said by the lord chauncellor Chief Justice & Attorney Generall.

Also this gent was to lie in prison till he willinglie resigned to the King by writing his said order & patent : the like president was before in Sir Antonie Shurley's [1] & Sir Alexander Clifford's cases.

This parliament has desired the reviving of an act of 23 H. 8 that no French wyne should be brought into England betwene

---

[1] Sir Anthony Shirley and Sir Nicholas (not Alexander) Clifford, two of the bravest and most gallant officers of the English auxiliaries, were invested by Henry IV. of France with the Collar of the Order of St. Michael. On their return to England they were committed to prison by Elizabeth for daring to accept this honour without having previously obtained permission of the Queen's Grace, and were peremptorily ordered to send back the Collar (Wicquefort's

Michaelmas & the Purificacion of our Ladie: wherin was concluded in the debate that the wyne about Burdeux, which is the smallest wyne, is ther apointed first to be sold: & then after Christmas come downe thither from the high countreys the better wyne & better chepe.[1]

Yet our merchants are so desirous to buy at the first & the French so desirouse of the first sale as they sell wyne, that want tyme, of unripe grapes, & that hath not had 20 daies: in that tyme it might purge: which makes the wyne unholsome & quicklie sower: wherin doctor Paddie[2] said the best wyne was of the second leaz, meaning two yeres old: before which tyme it is unperfect.

He saieth Columella & Varro write in old tyme wyne under 4 yeres old was called new wyne: after till 7 it was ripe wyne: & after 7 yeres it was old wyne.

The French merchants that should fill the vessels, that by heate it might purge out the putrefacion [for the rolling by sea geves it heate, & so when it is new the heate makes it purge], they doe not fill up the caske—so that the putrefacion remaynes in the caske—to save so much of the wyne: & when it hath wrought, tho the putrifacion for want of filling doth not worke out but remaines in, then with 14 barrels they mak up tenne & so sell naughtie wyne.

But cold frosts trie the goodnes, for after Candlemas by tast, savour & colour it may easilie be deserned to be bad wyne that in lesse then a sommer will either stink or be sower.

Therfore the best buying wyne is after Januarie at the second vintage that comes in.

This xi of *March* 1606, the Lords & Commons had conference touching a bill passed by the Commons against purveyours: wherin it was sett downe that redie money & markett prises should be paid for all achates: & for carts such prises as Justices of peace sett downe: & the seller & the constable to be present at the takinge: & ther commission of purveiors to be made acording to all the lawes, to be shewed at the taking, or els the purveyors to

Embassador and his Functions, p. 354; *S.P.Dom.* 1591–4, p. 484; and *Dict. Nat. Bio.*).

[1] This Bill was read for the third time on March 31, 1606 (*C. J.* i. 291).

[2] Sir William Paddie, M.P. for Thetford (*Parl. Hist.* i. 974); Fellow of College of Physicians, 1591; President, 1609–11 and 1618; knighted 1603; Physician to James I. (Foster's *Alumni Oxonienses*, Early Series, vol. iii.).

be felons : also the Greneclothe not to iudge those causes but the
courts at Westminster.

The attorney first, & after the Lord Chief Justice in the name
of the rest present, & with consent of the Lords, shewed that this
wold hinder the king 50,000[1] per annum,[1] to take away the king's
prerogative in purveiance which is saved expreslie in a statute 27
E. 3 :[2] also the chief Justice said the king had prerogative in
purveyance to have it at a more reasonable prise then the markett
prises : as first for some things the prises had ben alwaies certen,
which the attorney said were mencioned in the old Grene Clothe
bookes to be hereditarie prises : also the chief Justice cited record
in Westminster courts also in E. 3 tyme, wherin it was adiudged
that the king in corne was to have of the subiects 21 bushells for
20, & of strangers 22 by . . . for 20 : & another recorde that the
king was to have ech 8 bushell heaped. Also the king had a prerogative to have such prises, as had contynewed 100 or more yeres :
& when no certen prise had ben, ther on even apraizment, not to
high to charg the king nor to baze to opresse the pore : & if the
king had no favour in the price, but a bare preempcion, the collecion of his provision wold farre excede the markett prise in
charges : the attorney said no statute prohibited purveyance, but
punished undue purveiors : & adiudged that timber groyng being
frehold no(r) children that lerned singing for plesure no takes.
The statutes that apoint present payment have ben expounded, by an
act 4 H. 4 [3] in the Tower,[4] to be as sone as the king hath money :
onlie things under 40[s] had present payment by the old statuts.

They said that wher the bill [5] made it felonie to take without a

---

[1] In 1604 the Lords at a conference had proposed an annual grant of 50,000*l*.
in lieu of Purveyance (Gard. *Hist.* i. 173).

[2] 27 Ed. III. St. 2, *De Stapulis*, cap. iv., which, while exempting those going to
and from the Staple from disturbance by purveyors, saves the King's prerogative
to exact from them ' toutz maners des prises Roialx dez cariages et Vitailles .
auncienment dues et uses de droit, come ad este fait par nous et nous auncestres '
(*Stat. at Large*, i. 269).

[3] Not ' 4 ' but 2 Henry IV. c. 14, enacted that purveyance for the King's house
of 40*s*. or under shall be presently paid for (*Stat.* i. 404).

[4] Wilbraham was for a time Keeper of the Records in the Tower (*S. P. Dom.*
1603-10, p. 15) : but Mr. Hubert Hall, of the Public Record Office, kindly informs
me that his patent was vacated after hearing by the Council in 1604 as an infringement of the rights of the Master of the Rolls.

[5] The Commons' present Bill.

commission of purveiance acording to the severall statuts, the lawes were 36 of Purveiors : [1] some abrogating other by generall & some particular words & implicacion : the lawes were so intricate that 6 the best lerned in 6 mouthes could not drawe a commission : & so the act therin to make it felonie was to rigorous.

Also to abrogate the grenecloth, which tho it were no court of record yet the necessitie of the king's present service required that they might & used lawfullie to punish by imprisonment such as resisted lawfull purveyance.

14 *April*, The Lords upon sute granted conference to the Commons, touching ther desires in ecclesiasticall causes : [2]

1. They desired that 300 ministers, deprived for not subscribing, might be licenced to prech, being all meanes they had to live upon : especiallie such as nether sought to sett up a presbeterie, or desired a paritie, or were of turbulent spirites : the desired tolleracion for these present, & not for future tymes : & since domb ministers were not deprived of anie living, ther contempt of not subscribing ought not to tak away not onlie the present livings, but also ther preching within these daungerous tymes, when practizes of poperie are everywher busie to deprave & seduce the people : & in Elizabeth tyme lawes were a terror to Rome (?) : but inflicted upon some that were not turbulent : thes speches were devided in 10 partes & eloquentlie handled by Sir Frauncis Bacon ·

2. Sir Henry Hobert [3] desired for the commons that the eccle siasticall commission might not be executed but in London & York : 1° for that it was an arbitrarie & absolute authoritie : 2° it was without apelle : 3° it abrogated from the ordinarie jurisdicion, & hindred the chauncelour of bishops lerned in civill lawe : 4° besides excomunicacion, it authorizeth fines & imprisonments without limitacion of tyme or some : it was the highest commission & authoritie next parliament : & by this a parti may accuse himself :

---

[1] The Commons had declared, in May 1604, that the grievances in purveyance, of which they complained, had been declared to be illegal by no less than thirty-six statutes (Gard. *Hist.* i. 172).

[2] Mr. Spedding gives an account of this conference, collected from the Commons' Journals (*Letters and Life of Francis Bacon*, iii. 263, &c.), but Wilbraham's report is somewhat fuller.

[3] Sir Henry Hobart, appointed Attorney-General July 4, 1606, and Chief Justice of the Common Pleas 1613.

therfore to be committed to men of preeminence for integritie, iudgment & experience: to be executed in a publik place, and not in bishops chambers: to be assisted with men of equall credit: & not the bishop with his chaplens to geve sentences, which were *penes unum*: to be executed nere London & York, wher councellors might advise & prevent errors.

Sir H. Montague [1] desired citacion, acording to the Statute of Westminster 2, might conteyne the causes & the accusors in every matter: & not to send out a *quorum nomina* for 40 at a time, & then to compell them to take an oath to accuse themselves, which is against all lawes in causes criminall

Lastlie M[r] Sollicitor Doderidge [2] made an excellent spech to move that excommunicacion should not be upon triviall causes, for non aparances the first day, for a bundell of leekes: it was against the auncient canons & cited the text that that punishment was the last & most heynous, & excommunication was *exclusio a sacramentis, a sacris et communione fidelium*: & therfore by the canons not to be inflicted but by extreme necessitie: these speches were amplified with allegories & elegant sentences, an howre & half, & most aproved of all the temporall lords by ther silence admiring the eloquence & witt of the spekers: & the archbishop desired tyme to answare in so weighti a cause.

The lords after often debate refused to ioyne in these 4 peticions to his maiestie: for touching the first, *melius est ut pereat unus quam civitas*: & without ceremonies religion could not be supported: for the 2nd, his Maiestie wold be cautious: & for the 4th, he purposed in place of excomunicacion to ordeine fine & imprisonment: for the 3rd, the bishops wold be carefull: & to all answare was that it was dangerous to have a peticion publik & scandalous.

15 *April*, The Commons, par Henry Yelverton et auter legisperitos, respond al argumentz folio precedenti pur prerogative	15 April. The Commons by Henry Yelverton [3] and other lawyers made reply to the arguments in favour of the King's

---

[1] Sir Henry Montagu, Recorder and M.P. for the city in 1603. Afterwards Chief Justice of the King's Bench in 1616, and Lord Treasurer in 1620 (Foss's *Judges*).

[2] John Doderidge, Solicitor-General, October 28, 1604; resigned office June 25, 1607, to give place to Bacon, and knighted; J.K.B. 1612 (*ibid.*).

[3] Henry Yelverton, eldest son of Christopher Yelverton, was M.P. for North-

le roy in purveyance : et ils arere fueront respond par Attorney a Chief Justice : 1° Commons et Judges varie in re un statute devant cite de 27 E 3, titulo statute staple, save prerogative le roy in prices, ou in prisage comme les commons diont : sed auters contra que ceo est prerogative de prices : ergo vide statute. Commons & Judges agree que Roy ad purveyance par common loy pur houshold : & act de parliament contra ceo est void, quia necessarie prerogative : & Judges diont que act que roy payer redie money est void : car roy doet aver iour de payment tanque il ad satisffie pur guerre, que est plus necessarie : et chief Justice dit que toutz prerogatives de roy sont allow pro lege pro bono publico. Commons et Attorney agree ove Judges et ii H 4, 3 H 4, et 6 H 3, titulo . . . . roy poet aver purveyaunce par force sil offer reasonable price : sed iudges diont ceo est price plus favorablement que markett : auterment charges de collecion sera plus grandes que subiectz pay :

prerogative set out in the preceding folio : and afterwards the Attorney and Chief Justice replied to them. 1. The Commons and Judges differ in regard to the Statute hereinbefore cited of 27 Edward III. entitled Statute of Staple,[1] the Commons saying that the King's prerogative is saved in prisage, while the Judges assert that it is his prerogative in prices which is saved : therefore see Statute. The Commons and Judges agree that the King has prerogative by Common Law for purveyance for his Household : and that an Act of Parliament against that is void, because it is a necessary prerogative : and Judges say that the Act that the King must pay ready money is void ; for the King ought to have a day for payment after he has satisfied war expenses, for that is more necessary : and the Chief Justice says that all the King's prerogatives are allowed on behalf of the law for the public good. The Commons and Attorney agree[2] with the Judges and Statutes 2 Henry IV, 3 Henry IV and 6 Henry III[3] that the King may have

---

ampton. He was reconciled with the King in 1609. In 1613 he was Solicitor-General, in 1617 Attorney-General, and in 1625 J. C. P. (Foss's *Judges*).

[1] 27 Edward III. *Vide ante*, p. 80 n.

[2] 2 Henry IV. c. 14. *Vide ante*, p. 80 n.

[3] There must be an error here, as there seem to be no statutes of these years relating to Purveyance. I cannot decipher or conjecture the word omitted.

purveyance by force if he offer a reasonable price ; but Judges say that means a price more favourable to him than the market price, for otherwise the King's charges of collection will be greater than those the subjects pay.

Lez commons relie sur 36 E 3, statute que est confirme par 23 H 6 : ceo act inter mults auters apoint que roy payer redie money & markett prices comme ieo remember : & mults statuts a ceo effect: sed auters antique leges sont que gree sera fait al subiects : & ceux sont void par iudges quia deniall de subiectz ne hinder le purveyaunce que est cy necessarie prerogative : le iudges attorney ne commons ne poent citer ascun case in ley que roy ad plus favorable prise in prisees que subiectz ont, ceo est markett prises, quel est expound comme commons diont reasonable prises. mes fuit controvert un statute de 27 E 3 devant cite et 36 E 3, que apoint covenable prises serra entier prises ou non : mes attorney & sieur chauncelor collect que nul execucion fut de ascun de ceux statutz pur reasonable prices : car lez commissions de south le grand seal pur prisage & purveyaunce mencione de temps H 7 ont reasonable &

The Commons rely on the Statute 36 Edward III,[1] which is confirmed by 23 Henry VI[2] : that act among many other things ordains that the King is to pay ready money and market prices, if my memory serves me right : and there are many Statutes to the same effect : but there are other ancient laws ordaining that grace should be given to the subject : & yet they are void according to the Judges, because the denial of the subject does not prevent purveyance in so much as it is so necessary a prerogative : Neither the Judges nor the Attorney nor the Commons can cite any case in law that the King has a more favourable price in prises than subjects have ; that is the market price, which is interpreted according to the Commons to mean reasonable prices. But this view was controverted by the Statutes 27 Edward III hereinbefore cited and 36 Edward III, which ordain suitable prices, that is prices

---

[1] 36 Ed. III. st. i. cap. 2-6. *Stat. at Large*, i. 297.

[2] 23 Henry VI. cap. i. *Ibid.* p. 534.

royal prises : & le execucion prove le intent de leges : auxi lez acomptes in eschequer de toutz royes prove que heaped measure ad ete pay al roy & acomptes answare ceo : est un prerogative certen par statute pur prices de vyne tantum : & par *Magna Charta* un price certen pur cart & 2 chevals est 10^d, sed pur petit choses certen prises ont este par usage.

Et pur bief & mutton & grand choses prises sont variable sed favorable pur roy acordant al temps :

Le iudges agree que grenecloth nest court, forque de punish ceux quex deny ou resister purveyaunce : et in ceux cases tantum ils imprison : et comment *Magna Charta* est que *super nullum ibimus nec mittemus nisi per legem terrae* : uncore in ceo case ceo est lex terrae : sicomme courtz de equitie &

without reserve or none. But the Attorney and Lord Chancellor show that these Statutes for reasonable prices have never been actually made use of, for the Commissions under the Great Seal for prises and purveyance mentioned from the time of Henry VII contains the words, ' reasonable and royal prises : ' and the fact that the commissions have been thus issued proves the intention of the laws. Also the accounts in the Exchequer of all the Kings prove that heaped measure has been paid to the King, and the accounts show that. For prices of wine there is a certain prerogative by Statute : and by Magna Charta the fixed price for a cart and two horses is 10^d,[1] but for little things the prices are fixed by usage.

And for beef and mutton and great things the prices vary · yet are they favourable to the King according to the time.

The Judges agree that the Greencloth is not a Court : except to punish those who refuse or resist purveyance : and in these cases only they imprison ; and although Magna Charta ordains ' upon no man will we go nor send unless by the law of the land ; ' yet in that case that is the law of the land, just

---

[1] Henry III., reissue of *Magna Charta*, 1216 (*Select Charters*, p. 342.)

Starchamber, quex examyne person sur lour serment, et councell table, comment ils nont legall & formal procedings,—uncore est per legem terrae : mes si grenecloth erre ou imprison ascun contra leges, le iudges de lez grant *Habeas Corpus* de examiner lour procedings & deliver le parti sur case : & in conclusion fuit dit que comment le strictnes de bill verz purveyours (que fuit direct par auncient statute nient mise in use) fuit strict verz prerogative de roy que lie luy al markett prises, & redie payment, et de extinguishe le greneclothe : uncore le roy entend ease de people par proclamation, in prices & in takings & dabatur nomber de cartes, &c : quod det deus. Et proclamation fuit fait que in part prevent extorcions taking que ne fuit imploy par roy.

as the Courts of Equity and Starchamber, which examine persons on their oath, and the Privy Council, although they have no legal and formal procedure, yet are they according to the law of the land. But if the Greencloth err or imprison any one against the laws, the Common Law Judges grant writs of Habeas Corpus, so that they may examine into their proceedings and deliver the party on the case. And in conclusion it was said that although the bill against purveyors (which was directed by ancient Statute never put into use) was strict against the prerogative of the King, binding him to market prices and ready money payment and abolishing the Greencloth, yet the King intends the ease of his people by proclamation in all prises and taking : and the number of carts required shall be given : May God grant that this will be. And a proclamation was made that in part prevents extortionate takings from being employed by the King.[1]

5 *maii* Al councell bord · limposicion de 5ˢ 6ᵈ cwt currantz fuit peticioned against : et le sieur Chancelour chief Justice et Attorney diont que roy sur

5 May at the Council Board : The impost on currants of 5ˢ 6ᵈ the cwt was petitioned against ; and the Lord Chancellor, Chief Justice, and Attorney General

---

[1] The proclamation, though it put an end to most of the abuses, left untouched the claim of his officers to settle at their pleasure the prices they would give (Gard. *Hist.* i. 299.)

ceo foren commoditie, especialment comme chief Justice dit
estant vanitie, poet impose ascun
novel custom : issint royne
Marie impose 5ˢ sur chescun
clothe, par proclamation : et roy
sese le currantz tanque ley
trie in le point : et merchantz
contra diont, que le custome de
currantz est 5ˢ 6ᵈ in Venice :
et 18ᵈ auncient custome de
Engleterre et ore est increase
de chescun cwt a 5ˢ 6ᵈ et farme
al sieur chamberlaine : que issint
subiects pay circa 1ᵈ ob pur
chescun pound : et ce est grevance in parliament. Auters
grevances fueront propone in
parliament : 1° ce de currantz :
2° grant al Sieur Danvers de
toutz issues reconizances per
Angliam : 3° simile al Sir H
Broncar per Walles : 4° simile
al Sir Roger Aston pro Duchi
Lancaster : 5° licence de blockwood al Sir Arthur Aston : 6°
custom de new draperies al
Duke Lenox : 7 licence de re-
taile vynes al sieur admiral :
8 licence de blew starche : 9
imposicion de sea coles : 10

say that the King can impose
any new custom on that foreign
commodity, especially, as the
Chief Justice says, when it is
a luxury. Thus Queen Mary,
by proclamation, laid an impost
of 5ˢ on each piece of cloth.
And the King may seize the
currants until the matter is
decided in the Courts.[1] And
the merchants on the contrary
say that the duty on currants
in Venice is 5ˢ 6ᵈ, and 18ᵈ was
the ancient duty in England
and now it is increased to 5ˢ 6ᵈ
on each cwt and farmed to the
Lord Chamberlain :[2] So that the
subjects pay about 1½ᵈ on each
pound : and this is a grievance
in Parliament. Other grievances
were put forth in Parliament.[3]
1. this impost on currants; 2.
the grant to Lord Danvers of
all the issues from Recogni-
sances throughout England ; 3.
grant of the same to Sir H.
Brounker[4] throughout Wales ;
4. grant of the same to Sir
Roger Aston[5] for the Duchy of
Lancaster ; 5. the licence of
blockwood to Sir Arthur Aston ;[6]

[1] This had been done in Bate's case.　　　[2] Earl of Suffolk.

[3] In the Petition of Grievances presented in the session ending May 27, 1606. For these Grievances and the King's reply thereto at the opening of the next Session, see *post* and *C. J.* i. 316–17.

[4] Sir Henry Brounker, President of Munster, after Carew.

[5] Sir Roger Aston, Gentleman of the Bedchamber (*S. P. Dom.* 1603–10, p. 65, Jan. 9, 1604). Master of the King's Great Wardrobe in 1608. (*Ibid.* p. 460.)

[6] Sir Arthur Ashton : licence to him and others for forty-one years to use and sell certain woods used in dyeing, Aug. 23, 1604. (*S. P. Dom.* 1603–10, p. 146.)

licence de transport ordinance :
11 saltpetre : 12 preempcion of
tynne : & 3 auters : roy promise graciousement a reformer
oppression et abuses : mes ad-
monishe quils ne derogate de
son prerogative : et pro maiori
parte ceux grants sont petit
damages al people, et grand
profitt pur subsistance de corone :
quaere eventum.

6. the duties on new draperies
to the Duke of Lennox ; 7. the
licence of retailing wine to the
Lord Admiral ; 8. the licence of
blue starch ; 9. the impost on
sea coal ; 10. the licence of
transporting ordnance ; 11. saltpetre ;[1] 12. the preemption of
tin : and three others. The
King promised graciously that
he would reform oppressions and
abuses, but warns them that they
do not derogate from his prerogative, and for the most part
these grants are of very little
damage to the people ; and of
great profit towards the support
of the Crown : Query as to the
issue :

November : 1606 : Al auter
cessions de parliament : le
chauncellor notifie al commons
que roy ad ove son councell
consider de ceux grevances : et ad
respond a chescun particulerlie,
et les grants al Sieur Davers,
et auter al Sir Arthur Aston
fueront repelle : mes les privi-
lidge et imposicion de currants
adiudg bone in eschequer : et
les auters sont affirme bone par
prerogative de roy a granter :
vide le peticion de commons et
respons le roy al ces cessions.

November 1606 : At the
other Session of the Parliament.
The Chancellor[2] notified to the
Commons that the King has
considered these grievances with
his council ; and has replied to
each particular ; and that the
grants to Lord Danvers and to
Sir Arthur Aston were repealed ;
but the privileges in the matter
of currants and the impost
thereon were held good in the
Court of Exchequer :[3] and the
others are affirmed good by
reason of the King's prerogative

---

[1] Patent to John Evelyn and others for making saltpetre for supplying the King's
gunpowder for twenty-one years, Oct. 7, 1604 (*S. P. Dom.* 1603_10, p. 156). The Evelyn
family carried on the manufacture of gunpowder at Long Ditton and Godstowe.

[2] Nov. 18, 1606, on   opening of the autumn session (*C. J.* i. 314–15).

[3] Bates's Case, decided Mich. Term, 1606.

Auxi le chauncellor promise pur roy spedie payment de privie seals hors de subsidies : et le primer defection happen pur ceo le subsidie fuit plus petit que ascun assegnment : et trop tarde in payment.

to grant them. See the petition of the Commons and the King's reply thereto this Session.

Also the Chancellor promises for the King speedy payment of the Privy Seals out of the Subsidies ; and the first defect in payment arose by reason of the Subsidy being smaller than any assignment, and being paid too late.

Et sur ceo le roy urge le union comme le sole matter destre treat in ceo cession : et respond al obiections.

And therefore the King urged the Union [1] as the sole matter to be treated of in that session : and replied to the objections.

1° Est dit que nest necessarie destre enact quia il et chauncelor diont, le unitie de soveraigne fait unitie in subiectes : sed order in ceo unitie est destre declare pur avoid inconvenience par certen limitacions et rules.

1. It is said that it is unnecessary that it should be enacted, in as much as the King and the Chancellor say that the unity of the subjects is involved in the unity of the Sovereign. But order is to be observed in setting forth this unity by establishing definite limitations and rules, so as to avoid inconvenience.

2° Obiect que Scotland est pore et England riche : ce nest reason de devide Gales de Engleterre : ergo nec icy : auxi riches ne fait realme famous ou honorable, sed le communion et participation de ceo al plusors fait enlargment de kingdome ·

2. It is objected that Scotland is poor and England rich. But this is not a reason to divide Wales from England, therefore it is not one here. Also riches do not make a realm famous or honourable, but the communion and participation thereof among many enlarges a Kingdom.

---

[1] The King's speech on the Union is fully given in the *Parliamentary History* (i. 1071-5), taken from the *Commons' Journals*.

3° Roy borne in Scotland est parcial a eux : son conversacion declare le contrarie : et il ne serra ingrate al England, nec unnatural al Scotland : et il ne unques committ que serra dit que roy de Scotland serra inimy al roy dengleterre : et le person le roy et le ley serra icy.

Pur le union il desire ceo pur equal benefit dambideux : est rare quil ne fait, quant poet estre fait sans parliament par le roy ·

Toutz realmes in amitie ont commerce, plus tost ceux deux quex ont un roy : et subiects nee avant sont naturalls de ambideux comme iudges ont declare : ceux nee postea, que ceux fueront unite in le roy et son person : auxi North Britten unite al South comme Wales al Engleterre serra strenth pur resist invasion : auxi in future ils serra rule par un ley : et serra ioyous mariage.

Ce union particular terror al enimies : et mettre dissention serra scandalous : union est essence de dieu, peace de ment et bond de mariage : sed nil fuit conclude in ces 40 iours de cession.

3. The King born in Scotland is partial to the Scots. But his conversation shows the contrary : and he will never be ungrateful to England or unnatural to Scotland. And he will never act so that it shall be said that the King of Scotland will be the enemy of the King of England.

Moreover the King's person & his Courts of Justice will be here in England. He desires the Union for the equal good of both. It is wonderful that he does not bring it to pass, when it can be effected without Parliament by the King himself.

All realms in amity have commerce ; still more those two realms who have one King. And subjects born before the King's accession, naturalized in both realms, as the Judges have declared ; and those born after his accession are united in the King and his person. Also North Britain united to South Britain as Wales is to England will be made strong to resist invasion. Also for the future they will be governed under one law : and there will be a joyous marriage.

This union will be a special terror to our enemies ; and it will be scandalous to set up dissention. Union is of God's essence, peace of mind and bond of marriage. But nothing was concluded in the forty days of this Session.[1]

7 *Sept:* Councell assemble private pur suplie grand defect de treasure.

Et in *Nov:* fuit offer par customers de lend al roy 1200000[1] sur lour rent devant pur customs : issint si roy ded que dieu defend; farmers in peril de perdre : uncore par perswacion de Councell fut aprompt al roy : sed le roy pay interest *ut opinor:* et 80000 aprompt de Londoners sui private perswacion de Councell de repayment.

7 Sept.[2] Council assembled privately in the matter of the great defect of the Treasury.[3]

And in November the farmers of the Customs offered to lend the King £1,200,000[4] on their rent, before the negociations for the customs were completed; so that, in the event of the King's death, which God forbid, the farmers were in danger of losing—yet by the persuasion of the Council the loan was advanced to the King; but the King pays interest, as I think. And the citizens of London lend £80,000[5] on the private persuasion of the Council that it should be repaid.

Med. June 1607 : beggars et

In the middle of June

---

[1] The Session adjourned *Dec.* 18, 1606.   [2] 1607.

[3] During the year ending with Michaelmas 1607 the expenditure had risen to 500,000*l.*, while the revenue, even with the addition of the grant made in Parliament, only reached 427,000*l.*, leaving a deficit of 73,000*l.* (Gard. *Hist.* ii. 12). The debt at the beginning of 1606 stood at 774,000*l.* (vide *ante,* p. 76).

[4] *Sic* : but probably a mistake for 120,000*l.* See warrant dated Feb. 22 1607, for renewal of lease to farmers of customs of tonnage and poundage on their augmenting the rent from 112,400*l.* to 120,000*l.* p. a. (*S. P. Dom.* 1603_10, p. 349), and warrant dated Nov. 5, 1608, to repay to Sir Thomas Hayes, Sir Baptist Hickes, and others of London 120,000*l.* lent by them to the king with interest thereon (*ibid.* p. 465).

[5] See warrant dated March 21, 1608, wherein is included the payment of 80,000*l.* with interest, borrowed of divers citizens and merchants, strangers of London (*S. P. Dom.* 1603_10, p. 415). A repayment on June 24, 1609, of 77,072*l.* 8*s.* 4*d.* for a loan from Sir Henry Rowe, the late Lord Mayor (1607), and other citizens, apparently refers to this (Devon's *Exchequer Issues of James I,* pp. 92–93).

vagarants in Northampton Vill in despite dencloser fait prope le ville par bandes in le nuite disclose part de ceo: quil ne estant represse nombers increase de ce towne & divers villes in ceo countie et in counties de Warwick, Leicester &c.: et per 20 iours increase lour nomber: ut 300 ou plusors in un lieu *per dies et noctes* succide les novel inclosures et ne desist tanque 2 proclamations, a several temps fait par le roy quils aver iustice: et merci sils desist: et uncore ils continew tanque Sir A. Mildmay et auters horsemen ove force et slaughter de ascun 10 in hott blond: ils fueront represse. Apres in lassise de severall counties avant dit 2 ou 3 fueront suspend pur example: ut roy dit *ut pena ad paucos metus ad plures perveniat*: et nest loyal action, les proclamations diont, pur subiects de reforme lour grevances par force: mes par peticion al roy destre relieve in iustice: et les Justices dassise pur satisfaction de baze people invey vers inclosers et depopulators: et inquire de eux et promise reformacion par iustice: que ad

1607: Beggars and vagrants in the town of Northampton, angered at the enclosures made near the town, in bands during the night threw down a part thereof. And in as much as they are not put down—their numbers increase, both from this town and divers towns in the county and in the counties of Warwick, Leicester, &c., and for 20 days their numbers continne to increase, till 300 or more in one place night and day are throwing down the new enclosures, nor do they desist in spite of two proclamations made by the King on different occasions that they should have justice and mercy if they desisted.[1] And yet they continue until Sir A. Mildmay [2] with some horsemen using force slay some ten in hot blood; and thus they were put down. Afterwards at the assizes of the before mentioned several counties, two or 3 were hanged as an example. So that, as the King says, the punishment of a few may impress the majority with fear. Moreover the Proclamation says that it is not a legal course for subjects to

---

[1] There are letters among the Hatfield MSS. showing the King's anxiety on behalf of the poor in this affair (Gard. *Hist.* i. 355 n.).

[2] Of Apethorp; eldest son of Sir Walter Mildmay, Chancellor of the Exchequer to Elizabeth. Antony had been Ambassador from the Queen to Henry IV. in 1596. James I. dined at his house in 1603 on his way to Sir Oliver Cromwell's at Hinchingbrook, died 1617 (Bridge's *Northamptonshire* (ed. Whalley), ii. 427, 587).

animate le people : quils threaten par muttering manner de aver plus violent revenge sils ne releve : sur que le Councell apoint selected commissioners in 6 counties ascun erudite in ley, de enquire de depopulacions et de convercion de arable in pasture : quex report al councell table 6 *Dec:* 1607 a cet effect que in counties de Lincolne, Lecester, Northampton, Warwick, Huntingdon, Bedford et Buckingham circa 200 ou 300 tenements depopulated: et grand nomber de acres scilicet 9000 in Northamptonshire : et grand nomber in auters counties converte de arable in pasture : et que people desire lour commons partenant ad villes destre disenclose: quil point ne fuit inquire par commissioners mes est referre al ley : et les depopulators offer reformacion et submitt eux al merci de roy : et ned al merci Sir H. Carey patenti de penal statute vers depopulators ·

remedy their grievances by force, but that they should petition the King to be relieved according to justice. And the Judges of Assize in order to satisfy the common people inveigh against Enclosers and Depopulators ; and inquire concerning them and promise reformation at the hands of Justice. And this puts courage into the common people, so that with mutterings they threaten to have a more violent revenge if they cannot be relieved. On this the Council appoints select Commissioners, learned in the law, in the six counties ; to inquire concerning the acts of depopulation and conversion of arable into pasture land. And they report to the Council on Dec. 6, 1607, to this effect. That in the counties of Lincoln, Leicester, Northampton, Warwick, Huntingdon, Bedford and Buckingham about 200 or 300 tenements have been depopulated ; and a great number of acres have been converted from arable into pasture land. To wit, 9000 acres in Northamptonshire and a great number in the other counties. And that the people seek that their commons, appurtenant to the towns, should be disenclosed ; but this point was not inquired into by the commissioners, but is referred to the law. And the

Sur que fuit direct al lerned councell: que le plus notorious inclosers in chescun countie serra ce Christmas sommon al starchamber al Hillary terme: et la iustice et merci extend a eux, ne ils desparre et baze people insult et animate a fere rebellion: quel est grandment suspect. Auxi maior de Northampton Shirief et prochen Justices quex ne represse outrage initio serra auxi convent in Starchamber pur lour remissenes: et est hope que ce public example stay le furie de bazer people: quel consultacion ieo par commandement de councell report al roy al Newmarkett 8 *Dec.*: et il semble de allowe ceo course, pur manifestacion de son iustice: et spedi reformacion de opression et sieur Salisbury advise le depopulators et enormous inclosers quils submitt eux al roy, et redresse le offence present.

depopulators offer reformation and submit themselves to the mercy of the King, and not the mercy of Sir H. Carey,[1] patentee of the penal Statute against depopulators.

On this directions were given to the learned counsel that the most notorious enclosers in each county should be summoned this Christmas for Hilary Term before the Star Chamber: and justice and mercy shown to them, so that they should not despair, nor should the common people insult them or be incited to make rebellion, whereof they are greatly suspected. Also the Mayor of Northampton, the Sheriff and the neighbouring justices who did not repress the outrages at the beginning should also be brought before the Star Chamber by reason of their remissness. And it is hoped that this public example may stay the fury of the common people. These deliberations I reported to the King at Newmarket on Dec: 8th by order of the Council. And he seems to approve of this course, for the manifestation of his justice and the speedy reformation of oppression. And the Earl of Salisbury advises the depopu-

[1] Master of the Jewels, with his father, Sir Edward Carey (*S. P. Dom.* 1603–10, p. 15, June 21, 1603), and Gentleman of the Privy Chamber (*ibid.* p. 137, July 26, 1604); afterwards Viscount Falkland, 1620, and Lord Deputy in Ireland, 1622–29.

lators and enormous enclosers to submit themselves to the King, and make redress of the present offence.

Febr 1607 : Attorney declare que sur conference ove touts Judges, le ley vers depopulacion est cy variable et incerten que nul certen punishment poet estre vers eux comme vers converters de tillage in pasture, *pena est certen* : ergo fuit devise un commission a divers sieurs de councell iudges et masters de requests de compounder ove depopulators al entente de persuade eux a reedifie measons pur visible satisfacion al murmorant people, de pacifie eux ; potins que a gaine fynes al roy.

Feb. 1607 : The Attorney General [1] states that, after conference with all the Judges, the law against depopulation is so variable and uncertain that no fixed punishment can be inflicted on depopulators, as can be on converters of tillage and pasturage, where the punishment is fixed. Therefore a provision was made for a commission to issue to divers Lords of the Council, Judges, and Masters of Requests to make composition with the depopulators with the intent that they should persuade them to rebuild the houses with a view to giving visible satisfaction to the murmuring people ; and to satisfy them rather than gain fines to the King.

Ceux 2 precedant ans grand contencion ad este enter les Judges Westminster dun part: et Archcevesques et clergie et les presidentes de Wales et North et masters de requestes, pur ceo sur chescun sugestion & private mocion et pur gaine al courts et apres iudgment et sentences passe, pur delay pur grander part, prohibicions ont este agard

These two preceding years there has been great contention between the Judges of the Courts at Westminster of the one part ; [2] and the Archbishops and clergy, the Presidents of Wales and the Council of the North, and the Masters of Requests of the other part ; because on every suggestion or private motion and for the Courts' gain even after judg-

[1] Sir Henry Hobart.
[2] With Coke's accession to the Bench on June 30, 1606.

hors de bank le roy et le common bank de stay proceding al charge et grevence de sutors : meme complaint est par high commissioners et sieur admirall dengleterre : et roy ad blame eux et Fuller pleder committ pur sedicions et disgraceful parols de clergie authoritie destre papall : et sur ceo le prechers devant le roy et a Pawles & *alibi*, par allegories et ascun foits pleinment momordant *legis peritos* pur que ascuns out este punish par un iour *pro exemplo*.

ment & sentences have been pronounced, with a view to delay for the most part, prohibitions are granted out of the King's Bench and the Common Pleas ordering a stay of proceedings which causes expense and grievance of suitors. . The same complaint is made by the Court of High Commission and the Lord Admiral of England. And the King blamed them and Fuller,[1] a Pleader, was committed for seditious & disgraceful speeches against the authority of the clergy, saying that it was Papal. And on that the preachers before the King and at St. Paul's and elsewhere by allegories and sometimes even in direct words attacked the lawyers ; because some have been punished by a day having been assigned for their appearance before the court, as an example.

Ce devision enter clergie et temporal ley est de grand peril al state : ci bien comme le discontent de bazer people verz le gentri : sed dieu defend et continew son peace quel le pape desire de violate, par instigacions de papists de refuser le oath de allegeance :

This division between the clergy and the temporal law is full of great peril to the State, as much as the discontent of the common people against the gentry. But God defend and continue His peace, which the Pope desires to violate by instigating the papists to refuse the oath of allegiance.

Et pur avoider le opinion de

And for the avoidance of

---

[1] Nicholas Fuller, imprisoned by the High Commission Court in November 1607 for words used against its authority while pleading in the Court of King's Bench. For this contest see Gardiner's *History* (ii. 36–40).

cruelti : le roy le 15 de Febr.
command les Judges de user
grand discrecion in punishment
de priestes et recusants *ut pena
ad paucos metus ad plures per-
reniat* : et divers distinct rules
de limitt lour discrecion inde
fueront donne a eux.

Nota inde que in touts consultacions de grand councels un
doet attender le inclination de
president et secretaries quex
principalment direct eux : car
ils ont de roy secrett instructions
comment ascuns foits ils con-
ceale ceo : et ieo ay view un
letter de terror al Deputy et
Councell in Ireland, et letter de
moderacion al Deputie meme
secrett, in grand cases de peace
et guerre, et de religion la : &
plusors choses sont propound
prima facie al councell un voy
pur secrett purposes ou lenten-
cion de conclusion est auter :
ergo est perillous al councellor
al primer mocion, hastiment de
mettre son opinion : ou in cases
de moment destre precipitate in
execucion de rigorous leys : car
les Justices dassise quex execute
priests acordant al statutes
fueront blame sinon in cases ou
il est obstinate et wilfull papist
que inclyne auters a son superstition : et refuse le oath de allegeance devise par novel estatute :
car tiels recusants de ce sere-

being thought cruel, the King
(Febr. 15) commands the Judges
to exercise great discretion in
the punishment of priests and
recusants, so that by punishing
the few, fear may fall on the
many : and divers distinct rules
were given therein to them to
limit their discretion.

Note herein that in all deliberations of great councils one
should wait to see the wishes of
the President and Secretaries
who principally direct them ; for
they have secret instructions
from the King, although some
times they conceal it. And I have
seen one letter full of terror sent
to the Deputy and his Council
in Ireland, and another letter of
moderation sent in secret to the
Deputy alone, on important
matters of peace and war and of religion there : and many things are
put forth to the Council bearing
one construction on the surface,
for the purpose of secrecy, where
the intention is that quite a different conclusion shall be reached.
Therefore it is perilous for a
councillor, on the first motion,
hastily to put forward his own
opinion, or in cases of importance to be precipitate in the
execution of rigorous laws. For
the Justices of Assize who execute priests in accordance with
the Statutes are blamed, unless
it is a case of an obstinate and

ment sont daungerous entant que pape ad condemne ceux que acept le serement: issint sont confederates al pope comme le darraine letter par le roy declare.

wilful papist who inclines others to his superstition, and refuses the oath of allegiance, established by the new act. For such recusants who refuse the oath are dangerous; in as much as the Pope has condemned those who accept the oath. So they are confederates of the Pope, as the last letter of the King declares.

19 *April* 1608 : Erle de Dorsett grand Tresorer apres grand temps consume al councell table enter luy et Sir John Luson qui ad complaine al roy verz Tresorer pur countenancing de son nieces cause verz Luson & ascuns injuries fait *colore officii* comment in ley iustifiable : entendant daver Luson punishe pur ceo scandale : seiant al councell table et in serchant de paper de opinions de civilians pur redresse verz tiels accusors, in-

April 19, 1608. After long time spent at the Council table in a dispute between the Earl of Dorset, Lord High Treasurer, and Sir John Luson,[1] who had made complaint to the King against the Treasurer for his countenance of his niece's cause [2] against himself, and of certain wrongs done under colour of his office as if justified by the law; the Lord Treasurer, intending to have Luson punished for that scandal, while sitting at the

---

[1] Sir John Leveson, Kt., of Haling, Kent, M.P. for Kent in James's first Parliament, brother of Sir Richard Leveson, of Stafford (Hasted's *Hist. of Kent*, i. pp. 474, 8). Aubrey, referring to *Dorset's* sudden death at the Council Board, states that 'the trial was with this Sir Richard Temple's (*i.e.* his informant) great-grandfather.' Sir John Leveson's daughter Christian married Sir Peter Temple, of Stowe, the second Baronet, in 1630; their son Richard died in 1697, and his son, the fourth Baronet, also Richard, died in 1749 (Cokayne's *Complete Baronetage*, i. 82). Possibly, judging by the dates, Richard, the third Baronet, was Aubrey's informant, and for great-grandfather we should read grandfather. This would be the grandfather of Sir Richard Temple on the mother's side, Sir John Leveson, and not Sir Thomas Temple of Stowe, the first Baronet, his paternal grandfather or great-grandfather, as is stated in the note to the edition of Aubrey's *Brief Lives*, recently edited by Mr. Clark (ii. 211).

[2] Chamberlain, on February 6, 1607, writing to Carleton, refers to a cause in the Court of Wards between the Lord Treasurer and Sir John Leveson (*S. P. Dom.* 1603-10, p. 348).

stauter sans ascun notice ou foresight fell donne et instanter sans paroll parle obiit : estant terrible example & vulgar conceat que fuit iudgment de roy pur son hardnes de harte versus pauperos, il estant infinite welthie et trop grand husband pur corone ut populus fabulat : sed fiat exemplum aliis : car est example de terrible iudgment de dieu.

Council table and in the act of searching for a paper containing an opinion of civilians concerning redress against such accusers, suddenly, without any warning or prevision, fell down and instantly without a word spoken died. And this was a terrible example and in the opinion of the common people a judgment of the King for his hardness of heart towards the poor. For the Treasurer was exceedingly wealthy and too great a husband in the interests of the Crown, as the people say. But let it be for an example to others, for it is in reality an example of God's terrible judgment.

Infra 40 iours doctor Stanhop, civilian, obiit, estant de 40000[1] welth et de nul expence : sub cuius tumulo fuit escrit :

‘ a hundred & tenne lies under this stone :
a hundred to tenne to the devell he is gone.’

Within forty days Doctor Stanhope,[1] a civilian, died, worth £40,000 ; and miserly in his expenditure. On his tomb was inscribed—

‘ A hundred and ten lies under this stone,
A hundred to ten to the devil he's gone.’

Ce iour sieur Salisbury dit a moy que office de tresorer fuit un perilous place car sil consent al monopolies et al infinite devises pur concelement et novel

This day the Earl of Salisbury[2] told me that the Treasuryship was a perilous place, for if the Treasurer consents to monopolies and to all the numberless devices

---

[1] Sir Edward Stanhope, Chancellor of the Diocese of London.
[2] Salisbury became Lord Treasurer, May 4, 1608, on the death of Dorset (S. P. Dom. 1603-10, p. 427).

taxacions propone il procure malice de people et lour anathema : et sil resist serra fait odious al sutor et par case al roy.

for concealment and the pro posals of new taxation he gains for himself the people's illwill and their curses; and if he resists the same he will be made odious to the suitors (i.e. the monopo lists) and perhaps to the King.

June 1608 : Newes in court, out of Hell, that rich doctor Stan hope put a case to the divell: he said it concerned common law : & wold be advised by Sir John Popham : who said it was an eschequer cause & he wold put it to Dorsett lord Tresorer : &c.

Nota. Perion chief baron : Anderson chief Justice de bank, et Popham chief Justice *de banco regis*, senio confecti subito obierunt: Popham ayant prise pille de le empericke Rawlie, ayant signe plusors warrants meme heure, et estant in salute, instauter obiit.

It is to be noted that Periam [1] Chief Baron of the Exchequer, Anderson,[2] Chief Justice of the Common Pleas, and Popham,[3] Chief Justice of the King's Bench, worn out with age, suddenly died. And Popham had been in good health, but taking the pills of the empiric Raleigh [4] in the very same hour, just after he had signed several warrants, died suddenly.

Nota. Gawdy chief Justice de banke, estant le proper iudge de

It is to be noted that Gawdy,[5] Chief Justice of the Common

---

[1] Sir William Periam, Judge of the Common Pleas, 1581, one of the Commissioners appointed to hear causes in Chancery on the death of Sir Christopher Hatton, 1591, Chief Baron of Exchequer, and knighted January 1593, died October 9, 1604, aged 70 (Foss's *Judges*).

[2] Sir Edmund Anderson, Chief Justice of the Common Pleas from 1582 till his death, August 1, 1605, aged 75 (Foss's *Judges*).

[3] Sir John Popham, Chief Justice of the King's Bench 1592–1607, died June 10, 1607, aged about 76. He had presided at Raleigh's trial in 1603.

[4] Possibly Sir Walter Raleigh. The Queen had often gained benefit from his prescriptions, and a medicine was sent by him from the Tower, at her command, to the dying Prince Henry, the very day of his death (Gard. *Hist.* ii. 158).

[5] Francis Gawdy, named one of the Commissioners to hear causes in Chancery on the death of Hatton, 1591, Chief Justice of Common Pleas 1605, died 1606.

touts volunts, morust intestate:
& Hesketh attorney de gards
estant iudge de touts volunts,
obiit, son volunt, ut ipse fatebatur, nient perfect pro defectu
temporis:

Et Sir John Spencer le grand
merchant de Angleterre, ses
dettes et movables estime al
value de 100000¹, et ses terres
apres 14 ans estime al 12000¹
per annum, ad fait nul volunt et
supose ce fuit subduct: mes
sieur Compton qui marie sa file
et heire devient in lunacy: par
que tout movables fueront in
perill destre begge de roy: mes
le sieur Compton recover: et sic
prevent courtiers: sed verendum
ne sit improvidus: et sic ea quae
Spencer supra modum miser et
avarus acquisierit, subita largitione evanescant: ergo ne confide divitiis.

Pleas (before whom all wills
come), died intestate, and Hesketh,¹ Attorney of Wards, also
judge of all wills, died without
completing his will, owing, as
he himself confessed, to want of
time.

And Sir John Spencer,² the
great merchant of England,
whose debts and movables were
appraised at a value of £100,000,
and whose lands after fourteen
years were appraised at £12,000
per annum, has made no will;
and it was supposed to have been
removed secretly. But Lord
Compton, who married his daughter and heiress, became a lunatic,³
whereof all his moveables were
in peril of being begged of the
King. But the Lord Compton
recovered; and so prevented
the courtiers. But it is to be
feared that he is a spendthrift,
and so that which Spencer, inordinately miserly and grasping,
gained, by sudden lavishness will
vanish. Therefore put not your
trust in riches.

---

¹ Sir Thomas Hesketh, appointed Attorney of the Court of Wards April 15, 1597 (*S. P. Dom.* 1595-7, p. 390), knighted 1603, died in 1606 (*ibid.* 1603-10, p. 313).

² The great merchant and Lord Mayor of London, known as 'Rich Spencer.' His only child, Elizabeth, married William, second Lord Compton, against her father's wishes.

³ The inheritance, on the death of his father-in-law in 1610, is said to have turned Compton's head for a time (*Dict. Nat. Bio.*). In 1618 Compton bought his promotion to the earldom of Northampton with his wife's wealth (*Gard. Hist.* iii. 215).

Henry of France, the most famous warrior, a king' of gretest potency, magnanimitie, sagacitie & opulency, having newlie (for some unknowen attempt) erected & kept in regiments 50000 soldiers extraudinarie, & having 2 daies before with most costlie solemnitie crowned his queene,[1] & riding through Paris in his caroch, with 2 noble sitting by him; the caroch being a litle staied at a narow street: a baze fellow unknowen & of no regard, stept up upon the coach wheele, & with a knif long prepared for that purpose strok the king 2 blowes in his bodie, 1610,[2] wherby he died spechlesse afore he could recover the Louvier his pallace : & so he that had scaped so manie bulletts, & in manie & long warres had passed eminent & sondrie daungers, was thus soddainlie butchered by a pesant :[3] having so gret an army in the field as the like was never before, and so great an assembly at the coronacion, & in his chifest et populous citie : & the *plaudite* of his victorious raigne, was torned into a *plangite* to all Fraunce : to whom he lefte his sonne of 9 yeres age for ther kinge: his mother is his regent : & the welth he lefte is incredible : & no certen cause of his deth knowen, saving that a Jesuite confessor or Jesuitical books perswaded this unrepentant miscreant to kill the king for an expiacion of his wicked lief. *Sic transit gloria mundi.*

This spring 1610, at parliament which contynued 4 months[4] was propounded this king's great want of annual revenewe : his children['s] charges increasing &c : for which was required 200,000*l* annuall suport : & his debts protested by the Lord Tresorer to be 600000*l* :[5] for which was required a like supplie : which much amazed the commons : some offer was made of retribucions, as

[1] Mary de' Medici : appointed Regent on the departure of Henry IV. to join his army in Champagne.

[2] May 14, 1610.   [3] François Ravaillac.

[4] The session opened February 9, 1610, and was prorogued July 23. For this account by Wilbraham of ' the Great Contract' see *Parliamentary Debates* in 1610, edited by Dr. Gardiner for the Camden Society, vol. lxxxi., and his *History*, vol. ii. pp. 69-87.

[5] When Parliament had met in 1606 the debt stood at 774,000*l*. (*vide ante*, p. 76), or according to Dr. Gardiner at 735,280*l*. (Gard. *Hist.* i. 295.) The 600,000*l*. given as the debt by Wilbraham is differently accounted for in *Parliamentary Debates*, Salisbury, in his exposition of the condition of the Treasury at a conference on February 15, claiming that the debt had been reduced to 300,000*l*. (*Parliamentary Debates*, 1610, p. 5) ; while at another conference on February 24, i asking for a

taking away respite of homage : 2° binding the crowne to the tyme of 60 yeres limitacion : 3° cutting of penal lawes : 4° patents & pleding to be most favorabli expounded for the subiect : 5° no dett above 30 yeres continuance to be exacted : 6° all forfeted leases to be dispenced with : 6° no more imposicions to be henceforth laid upon home or foren commodities : 7° that Wales should not be subiect to such government as the king prescribe acording the power of the statute 32 H 8.[1]

These being considered by the commons, yet were they not embraced as things of so great value as the annual suport desired · but the commons finding the king's wants desired liberti to treat a contract for all prerogative tenures & ther incidents : namelie to extinguishe all wardships, liveryes, licence of alienation, respite of homage, & the court of wards, & inquisicions post mortem &c : & also to have all purveyance abolished (wherin the lawiers held we could hardlie have good assurance, doubting generalli the king's howse could not subsist without it) : & they did also desire th'other 7 profers to be included in the great contract : the king licenced the treatie ; & by his letter & oration of the lord Tresorer protested he wold not consent that any point of his soveraintie should be put in the contract : nether wold he assent except ther were offered in annuall support 140000[1] above the annual profits he made by wardes purveyaunce & other things : herupon it was debated into

supply of 600,000*l.*, he stated that 300,000*l.* was to pay off the debt, 150,000*l.* to furnish the navy, and 150,000*l.* to 'lie in his coffers for war or any just occasion' (*ibid.* p. 14). It must be remembered that Wilbraham was a member of this Par-liament and of the committee in conference with the Lords (*C. J.* vol. i. p. 393). Possibly also his old colleague at the Requests, Sir Julius Cæsar, now the Chan-cellor of the Exchequer, would furnish him with information.

[1] The Court of the Council of Wales was erected by *Statutes* 34 & 35 Henry VIII. c. 26 for that principality and its marches, with authority to determine such causes and matters as should be assigned to them by the King. It was claimed that the four counties of Hereford, Worcester, Gloucester, and Salop were included within the Council's authority as marches of Wales. This was controverted by the inhabitants of these counties, and was the subject of contention between the Common Law Judges and the President of the Council in the reign of James I. (Hallam, *Const. Hist.* vol. i. pp. 328-9, note.) Probably Wilbraham makes confu-sion here between the above statute and 32 Henry VIII. cap. 2, which is a Statute of Limitations. One of the grievances of the Commons was the rule ' *Nullum tempus occurrit regi*,' expressed in their demand that claims of the Crown should be limited to sixty years.

4 questions: 1° what shold be desired from the king: 2° what should be given by the subiects: 3° upon what lands or other things it should be levied, & how it might be equallie devided: 4° what assurance should be therof. The first was sett downe upon long debate in manie particulers: tho with reservacion to insert more *si quid ultra occurrit*: for the second 100000[1] per annum was willinglie offred: from thence by degrees & invencion, & after the house long weried were manie departed, it came to an offer of 160000[1]: from thence too 180000: & the king insisted upon 200000[1]: it was with reservacions assented to be that some: which some the king liked of, being often inculcate by the lord Tresorer that it must be a fixed & certen revenewe, which must in all be taxed wholie upon lands: when the commons ment that to be for a further debate & perchaunce to charge officers, usurers & merchandize with part of that tax: which was ever thought the land could not beare such an annuall charge for any long tyme: upon hope of sucesse in the contract, & in consideracion of the king's wants on[e] subsidie & 2 fifteenes [1] graunted *sed aegre*: so this cession ended: few things of moment enacted: & the parliament proroged [2] for 3 monthes onlie to the 9 of *October*; that in the interim it might be considered, how this support might be indifferentlie levied upon lands: for the rate of fiftenes is unequall & laid to much upon pore: 2° the rate of old rents most incerten & obsolete: 3° the rate of parsonages which is the 10th part is also unequall: 4° to tax all lands to the true exact rate, & then upon knowledge of all the land & acres in the kingdom & of the exact value & so to impose 2^d or 4^d in the pound, was the best waye: but non resolved on

In this cession, the commons desired redresse 1° that the latitude of the ecclesiastical commission might be limited: 2° that the subscripcion of the ministers might be but according to the statute of 13 Eliz: [3] 3° that the silenced & deprived ministers might be restored: 4° that the 4 English shires might be exempted from the iurisdiction of the Presidencie of *Wales*: & some other gre-

---

[1] Gardiner gives one subsidy and one fifteenth (ii. 82), but see *Parl. Debates*, p. 58.

[2] Parliament was prorogued on July 23, 1610.

[3] 13 Elizabeth, c. 13, enacting that all priests or ministers should subscribe to all the Articles of Religion which *only* concern the confession of the true Christian faith and the doctrine of the sacraments, comprised in a book entitled 'Articles whereupon it was agreed,' &c. (Hallam, *Constitutional History*, i. 192.)

vances. But the chief & gretest semed the new imposicions, by the Book of Rates[1] amounting to above 100000[1] *per annum*, might be taken away : for proef of the king's prerogative herin a late iudgment in theschequer chaumber[2] was alledged : & the lawiers of the commons after serch in the records brought president, that in former tymes some of those taxes by the kings were abrogated or confirmed by parliament, without whose assent the king as they wold perswade could not impose :

To these & other grevances the king at the last day gave some answares but not fullie satisfactorie.

At this cession in October : when after 3 weks spent they begane to treat of the great contract his Maiestie sent word,[3] he never en tended to yeld to the contract for support, unlesse he may have 500000[1] by supplie : wherby the commons never treated further of that contract, the most of them doubting, those great royalties were never entended to be abolished. After orations used by the Lords : & the first 7 points offred to the commons : & subsidies propounded, it was not thought fitt to put it to voices after manie daies debate : the commons alledged decay of staple commodities, inhauncement of all wares to be bought, the facilitie for favorites to spend the king's treasure, the imposicions upon merchandize wherof there is no limitacion, were the causes the people were not able to grant subsidies : so after 2 adiornements the parliament was proroged till 9 *febr* next :[4] no act concluded or resolved in 9 weeks cession : nether his maiestie nor commons satisfied in ther expectacions · *quod dii vortant in melius.*

Now for want of money the Lord Tresorer &c treat with the creditors, & such as have trusted officers, as the wardrobe &c.

Ther have ben commissions for sale & leasing lands : for defective titles : assart lands : establishing copiholders : conceled wards, contracting for wards :[5] & for fines of alienacion more strict then formerlie : increase of customes : silence from war & abatement of

[1] A *Book of Rates* had been published on July 28, 1608. The revenue from these new impositions is estimated at 70,000*l*. (*Parliamentary Debates* in 1610, Introduction, p. xx.)

[2] Bate's case, decided in November 1606.

[3] By the Speaker on November 5 (Gard. *Hist.* ii. 107). The 500,000*l*. was to pay his debts.   [4] Parliament was finally dissolved on February 9, 1611.

[5] Salisbury resigned to the King all personal profits derived from his office as

charges of Wardrobe & Household : yet are the king's charges by manie courts, & multitude of servants to himself, the Queen, Prince, Duke & Ladi Elizabeth : that want of money hath this yere 1611 occasioned 3 proiects :

1° a proclamation to enhaunce gold 2^s in the pounde, yet litle brought to the mint, because coinage is so deare of late : 2° about 90 knights of degrees called baronetts of inheritance next in place to lords : [1] & now ther is contencion for precedencie betwene them & barons' yonger sonnes : 3° a generall lone of money, wherby manie are retorned *infirmi* : & money like to be scarce : [2] god grant this lone may pay the crowne dett, supplie the Tower, provision magazons, & the navie : for no surplusage can be saved for any further preparacion for occasion of foren warre.

24 *May* 1612 died the erle of Salisberi, the lest Lord Tresorer in person [3] that ever was : but gretest in offices, for besides that place he was principall secretarie & master of Wards for Queen Elizabeth & King James : chauncelor of Cambridge : stuard to Queene and steward of Westminster, & Grenewiche &c : he more then a president was alpha & omega in Councell : he solie managed all foren affaires, especialli Ireland : he directed parliament : he managed all the revenew & gretest affaires of the King, Queen, Prince & Duke of York : he found the coffers emptie : yet by the invencions on the former page & that especiallie by inhaunsing the customs, for which he was much maligned, he supported the crowne 5 yeres : he built 3 incomparable howses [4] &c : of bountie in all expenses, magnanimous corage, infinite in witt & pollicie, admirable to all men in eloquence upon the sodaine : depe secrett & prudent in councell : and quid non : *deo servus mihi patronus.*

Master of the Court of Wards, and gave orders forbidding the acceptance of irregular payments from suitors (Gard. Hist. ii. 113).

[1] The title was offered to all knights or esquires possessed of lands worth 1,000l. a year on payment of 1,080l. in three annual payments. Within three years 90,000l. was thus obtained (*ibid*. ii. 112).

[2] In February 1611 the king granted to six favourites 34,000l. (*ibid*. ii. 111).

[3] Salisbury in person was much below middle height, probably not exceeding 5 feet 2 inches (Brewer's *English Studies*, p. 130).

[4] The Earl had the 'architectonic tastes' of his father, and in 1607, when he began the building of Hatfield, was also ornamenting and altering Salisbury House, in the Strand, and erecting a vast exchange, called 'Britain's Burse,' on the site of the present Adelphi (*ibid*. p. 114).

The last of *May* upon the Lord Tresorer's death the Chauncelor of Eschequer,[1] lord Tresorer's private remembrancer of the issues, & the clerke *pellis exitus et introitus*, delivered before the whole bodie of the councell privatelie (I beinge present) the state of the annual revenues in receates & expence : to this effect, viz. the yerelie receats *viis et modis* is 280000[1], the yerelie expences is 440000[1] : so as the issues exceade the yerelie receates 160000[1] per annum :[2] at which the councell cast downe ther heads, it being likelie the yerelie expence will dailie increase.

Besides the king's detts are nombred 500000[1] : wherof to the Londoners 110000[1] for money borowed : upon privi seales 140000[1] : to the Queue 42000[1]

THE CHIEF EXPENCES OF THE KING ANUALLY.

	l			l
1 household	100000.[3]		4 the Quene	20000.[7]
2 the Prince	40000.[4]		5 pencions	80000.[8]
3 navi & cordage	50000.[5]		buildinge	20000.[9]
robes & wardrobe	50000.[6]			

[1] Sir Julius Cæsar, April 7, 1606–1614.

[2] See Gardiner's *History* (ii. 199), based on Cæsar's notes, wherein the figures, the total debt and deficit are as here. The total receipts actually received every year were considerably larger, estimated in 1610, according to a paper prepared by Salisbury's directions before the meeting of Parliament, at 460,230*l*. (*Parliamentary Debates* in 1610, Camden Society, Introd. p. xx) ; but 280,000*l*. represents the regular and undisputed receipts of the Crown, derived chiefly from land or feudal revenue and customs, after setting aside payments which might not be repeated and such sources of revenue as the new impositions, estimated at 70,000*l*., and receipts derived from licenses of monopolies which produced in 1610 about 50,000*l*.

[3] In 1610 the expenditure of the cofferer of the household was estimated at 106,323*l*. (*Parliamentary Debates*, Introd. p. xii).

[4] Prince and Princess, 13,050*l*. (*ibid*.) ; but elsewhere Dr. Gardiner estimates the expenditure of the royal family in 1610, apart from the Queen, at 32,250*l*., or, in 1614, when Prince Henry was no longer living and Princess Elizabeth was married with a portion of 40,000*l*., at 26,000*l*. ('Comparative View of the Estimated Ordinary Expenditure of the Crown,' Gard. *Hist*. x. Appendix p. 222.)

[5] 40,000*l*. in 1610 (*Parliamentary Debates*, p. xii) ; in 1614 50,000*l*., as here.

[6] 24,616*l*. in 1610 (*Parliamentary Debates*, p. xii).

[7] 14,000*l*. in 1610 (*ibid*.) ; in 1614 24,500*l*. (Gard. *Hist*. x. 222.)

[8] 94,192*l*. is given to 'fees and annuities' in Dr. Gardiner's above-quoted 'Financial Tables,' *Hist*. x. 222.

[9] 24,000*l*. in *Parliamentary Debates*, p. xii.

Ireland anuall charge is besides the revenewe ther which
is *circa* 25000[1] . . . . 30000.[1]
(See note [2] as to Total.)

THE CHIEF OF THE REVENEW ARE FIRST

The customes	140000.[3]	Impostes of wine [4]	
The revenewe about	. 100000.	Duchy .	12000.[5]

profits of seals & fines in Courtes

			1
Alam rent .	8000.[6]	Court of Wards	20000.[7]
Ireland .	25000.		

Manie other parcels particularlie sett downe before the Lords in
writing : wherupon the councell fell into consideracion to rectifie
these defections.[8]

[1] 300,000*l*. in MS., but evidently a mistake for 30,000*l*. The total charge of
Ireland would thus amount to 55,000*l*. This nearly agrees with Dr. Gardiner's
estimate in 1610 in his 'Financial Tables,' *supra*, and in *Parliamentary Debates*
(Introd. p. xii), *i.e.* 52,584*l*., or 46,000*l*. in 1614, on the supposition that the 24,000*l*.,
the annual revenue of Ireland (Gard. *Hist*. ii. 112), is included in these totals, as
employed in Ireland to defray the expenditure.

[2] The total of the 'chief expenses' here noted is 415,000*l*., compared with
440,000*l*. stated above to be the yearly expenditure. But certain items are obviously
omitted: Dr. Gardiner reckons the total expenditure of 1610 as 517,547*l*., and of
1614 522,940 (Gard. *Hist*. x. 222).

[3] This must represent only the receipts from customs apart from the new im
positions, imposed in 1608 by the Book of Rates, which were reckoned to produce
annually about 70,000*l*. In Salisbury's estimate for 1610, already quoted, the
total customs, impositions set before 1608 (thus excluding the new impositions),
alnage, licenses, &c., are reckoned at 177,358*l*. ; or, deducting the alum rent
here given as 8,000*l*. and the imposts on wine amounting to about 23,000*l*.,
146,358*l*., whereof the great customs are set down at 120,000*l*. Thus we
arrive at approximately the sum of 140,000*l*. here given by Wilbraham for the
customs.

[4] The wine licenses in 1610 were estimated at 23,200*l*., *i.e.* sweet wines 6,000*l*.,
French and Rhenish wines 17,200*l*. (*Parliamentary Debates*, Introd. p. xix).

[5] In 1610 11,500*l*. (*ibid.*).   [6] 5,000*l*. in 1610.

[7] 24,000*l*. (Gard. *Hist*. ii. 112).

[8] The total of the items of revenue here given amounts to 305,000*l*. ; but here
again there are admittedly omissions. For the actual total revenue *vide ante*,
p. 107 note.

In *Nov.* 1612 died (of an ague caused by overheate in exercise at teniss as is thought) the noble prince Henry Prince of Wales,[1] to the great grief & losse of Great Brittaine. He was a hopefull prince 18 yeres old : & much lamented of all, because he had an heroicall spirite : stout & constant in his designes : obedient to the kinge : he kept his court in princelie state : in all his actions he shewed magnificence : he attended himself praiers & sermons att sett tymes, & tyed his servants therunto : he favored lerning & loved men of armes especiallie & all others of eminent qualitie : he favored & countenaunced his servants so much that made some to insult, that now stope : he was so provident in his expence & œconomy, that, as the master of rolles [2] tells me, he increased his revenew 6000 per *annum* : & left 9000 good debt to his maiestie : beside his iewels, plate, wardrobe, stable &c., of which his councell render an acompt to the king's councell. To conclude he was the chief gemme in the crowne & loadstar to all christian princes.

27 *Dec.* 1612 were espoused & contract the Counte Palatine of Reyne & the Ladie Elizabeth, sole daughter of King James, in the banketing howse in presence of his Maiestie & Councell & of manie honorable ladies & 300 courtiers & gentlemen more : the words of the contract was the same of that of mariage spoken publikelie in French by Sir Thomas Lake,[3] k[t], clerke of signet, a lay man : with a short blessing by the Archbishop of Canterberie for a happie successe : [4] it was comfortable to Protestants : yet maligned by Paptists : after 3 severall asking banes in the king's chappell, thes noble personage were maried together by the Archbishop of Canterberie 14 *Febr* 1612 [5] in the King's, Queen's & Prince's presence

[1] On October 10 the Prince was attacked by an illness which is now known to have been typhoid. On October 24, feeling somewhat better, he foolishly played tennis. A relapse set in, and on November 6 he died.

[2] Sir Edward Phelipps became Master of the Rolls on January 14, 1611, in succession to Lord Bruce of Kinloss. He was also Chancellor to Henry, Prince of Wales (Foss's *Judges*).

[3] Privy Councellor 1614, Secretary of State 1616. Lake read the contract in French with so bad an accent, and his translation was so absurd, as to raise general laughter (Gard. H*ist.* ii. 160).

[4] Abbott. His words were, ' The God of Abraham, of Isaac, and of Jacob bless these nuptials, and make them prosperous to these kingdoms and to His Church ' (*ibid.*). ' 1613.

in Whitehall chappell after a sermon ther: a great part of the nobilitie being ther & a rich & full courte, especiallie of females: & 3 severall maskes:[1] on[e] of the lords Courtiers: 2 other at 2 other nights from the Innes of Courte: the Court abounding in iewels & embroderie above custome or reason: God grant money to pay detts.

2 *Febr* 1612 on candlemas day[2] at night dyed Richard Wil braham of Nantwich, Esq[r], my father, whose second sonne I was: his age at his death was 88 yeres & 5 monthes:[3] of a strong voice, perfect memorie, & sound stomak to digest all grosse meates till his deathe: naturallie wise & politick: iust in all his dealings: verie liberal & charitable to the pore: never stayned with any deceat or notorious cryme: his chief care for 20 yeres was to see his grand child & heire[4] maried & setled to succeede him: but manie mocions & non succeded: his overeaching experience & long age made him ielouse of his yonger children & best freinds till the yere of his deathe: which semed to be hastened by reason of a fall, wherby tho not hurte yet made him languish in his bed 17 monthes & so as a candle whose oyle was spent died without payn god not giving him leave to see his beire maried, which was the whole care of his lief; like Abraham who after his toile never lived tho to see, yet not to dwell in Canaan the land of promise: so as man's wisdome or care will not prevaile to add one cubite to our stature.

4 *Feb*[r] 1612 : being 2 daies after his deathe Elizabeth Wilbra-

[1] (1) The Lords, (2) Middle Temple and Lincoln's Inn, (3) Inner Temple and Gray's Inn. The masque of the ' Inner Temple and Gray's Inn, which was the marriage of the Thames and the Rhine, devised by Sir Fras. Bacon, failed, the King being so weary and sleepy that he refused to see it till Saturday' (John Chamberlain to Alice Carleton, February 18, 1613, *S. P. Dom.* 1611_18, p. 170).

[2] February 2, 1613.

[3] Born August 13, 1528. Roger Wilbraham was his second son by his first wife, Eliza, daughter to Thomas Maisterson, of Nantwich, whom he married in 1550. See Ormerod's *Cheshire*, ii. 137, Pedigree of Wilbrahams of Townsend and Delamere Lodge, where the date of his death is wrongly given as February 6, 1612.

[4] Thomas Wilbraham, son of Richard, eldest son of the above (who died September 13, 1601), and nephew to Sir Roger. Thomas was born June 25, 1589; married, March 24, 1619, Rachel, daughter and sole heir of Joshua Clive, of Huxley, Cheshire. He was an esquire of the body to Charles I. *Died* 1643. (*Ibid.*)

ham, second daughter of me, Sir Roger Wilbraham, was maried in great St Bartholemew churche by Mr Westfield precher ther, in an assemblie of 4 knightes & divers gentlemen & others, to Thomas Wilbraham,[1] sonne & heire apparant of Sir Richard Wilbraham of Woodhey, knight,[2] chief of my name & kinred, by the father's side : & Thomas Wilbraham, being by his mother's side grandchild to Sir John Savage [3] of Cheshire, chief of my kinred by my mother's side : the grandfathers of both parties now decesed wishing that match in ther lief tyme, & my frends living much desiring that I having now no sonnes,[4] might with my daughter give to the chief of my name a part of my acquired inheritance : as god pleased I entend if god prevent me not : to whose blessing I humblie com mend the successe &c :

This Christmas 1613 the erle of Somersett did mary Fraunces daughter to the erle of Suffolke, she being latelie devorced from the erle of Essex *quia maleficiatus* : the pompe, state & greate guiftes & feastes exceded all example *quia placuit Regi*.

28 Jan : 1613 : fut committ al examinacion sieur Coke &c : si roy ad papal prerogative daver benefite que cardinal et evesques ont in prycing biens de mort	28 Jan. 161$\frac{3}{4}$. Sir Edward Coke was charged to examine whether the king has the papal prerogative of enjoying the benefit which Cardinals and

[1] Born about 1601, succeeded to the baronetcy, conferred on his father in 1621, in 1643, distinguished himself in the Royal cause during the Civil War, was fined 2,500*l.* and his estates sequestrated, died 1660. See Pedigree of Wilbrahams of Woodhey (Ormerod's *Cheshire*, iii. 380), and his monument in Acton Church (*ibid.* 349). When the marriage was solemnised at St. Bartholomew the Great the bridegroom was aged only about eleven and the bride about ten. Sir Roger Wilbraham is described as of St. John's, Clerkenwell. (See *Marriage Licenses issued by the Bishop of London*, 1611-1828, ii., Harleian Society Publications, vol. xxvi. p. 18.)

[2] Baronet 1621; married Grace, daughter to Sir John Savage; died 1643 (Cokayne's *Complete Baronetage*, vol. i. p. 163, where the name of the bridegroom's maternal grandfather is given as Thomas).

[3] Thomas Wilbraham, the bridegroom's grandfather, died in 1610 (*ibid.* p. 163), and Richard Wilbraham, the grandfather of the bride, died February 2, 1613.

[4] Sir Roger Wilbraham died July 31, 1616, leaving three daughters, coheirs to 4,000*l.* per annum (*S. P. Dom.* 1611-1618, pp. 390, 426 ; Ormerod's *Cheshire*, ii. 137, Pedigree of Wilbrahams of Townsend and Delamere Lodge).

homes : car fut beg : et agree quils nad quia nest loyal authoritie ; auxi stat 21 H. 8 ad extinct touts fees forque ceux petit la reserve.

Bishops have in prising the goods of dead men. For this right was sought. And it is agreed that he has it not because there is no legal authority for the same. Moreover the Statute 21 Henry VIII [1] has extinguished all fees in such cases save some small payments thereby reserved.

Auxi pur licenses de glasse est usual et loyal de grant monopolies de novel invencions que sont *pro re publica* : pur petit temps de 21 ans :

Also in reference to the licence to manufacture glass,[2] it is usual and legal to grant monopolies in the case of new inventions which are for the public good, for the short space of 21 years.

Roy intend de proclame son intent de leaser l'imposicions (?) ei qui plus dare voluerit : Auxi de proclame in Ireland son bone conceate de service son deputi ; estant in disgrace pur ceo commissioners ont examyne le extorcions & misfesans in government et trove luy sincere : ou ieo fui

King intends to issue a proclamation that he will lease the farm of the Impositions to the highest bidder. Also to issue a Proclamation in Ireland stating that he is well contented with the services of his Deputy,[3] who had been in disgrace, and whose alleged extortions and

---

[1] 21 Henry VIII. c. 5.

[2] This would seem to refer to a patent granted for the manufacture of glass with Scotch coal instead of wood, referred to in a letter from Suffolk to Lake, November 17, 1613, where Coke is mentioned as suggesting a new patent (*S. P. Dom.* 1611_18, p. 207); see also letter from Lord Chancellor Ellesmere to Lake, February 23, 1614, explaining cause of delay in putting great seal to patent (*ibid.* p. 224); and Chamberlain to Wake, October 12, 1614, where it is mentioned that the old patent is given up in favour of those who undertake to make glasses with Scotch coal (*ibid.* p. 256). The Commons made a grievance of it (Gard. H*ist.* ii. 237). Among the patentees were Sir Jerome Bowes and Sir Edward Zouch (*ibid.* 207).

[3] Chichester.

commissioner pur 4 moys ove Justice Winch, Sir ch Corne- wallies et M' Calvert, clerk de Councell : our procedings apere in our long certificate annexed to our commission under the greate seale of Ireland.

malfeasance in his government [1] had been the subject of exami nation by a commission. This commission, whereof I was a member for four months together with M' Justice Winch, [2] Sir Charles Cornwallis [3] and Mr. Calvert, [4] Clerk of the Council, found the Deputy upright. Our proceedings appear in our long certificate annexed to our com- mission under the Great Seal of Ireland.

Circa midsomer day [5] 1614: died th'erle of Northampton, [6] lord privi seale : who was glorious in his lief, yet now dead

[1] The long list of grievances charged against the Irish Government was deli- vered on July 15, 1613, though the commissioners did not arrive in Dublin until September 11. Their Report was sent in on November 12. The king delivered judgment on the charges on April 12, 1614 (Gard. Hist. ii. 295).

[2] Sir Humphrey Winch, Chief Baron of the Irish Exchequer 1606, Chief Justice of the King's Bench 1608, Judge of the Common Pleas (England) 1611_25 (Foss's Judges).

[3] Sir Charles Cornwallis, Resident Ambadassor to Spain 1605_9, Treasurer of Prince Henry's Household 1610 (Dict. Nat. Bio.).

[4] George Calvert, Secretary to Sir Robert Cecil, in 1606 Clerk of the Crown in the province of Connaught and county of Clare, in 1608 one of the clerks of the Council. From 1619 to 1625 Secretary of State, created Baron Baltimore 1625 (Dict. Nat. Bio.).

[5] June 15, according to Gardiner (Hist. ii. 259), who quotes a letter from Chamberlain to Carleton, June 30 (Court and Times of ames I. vol. i. p. 326). See also Larkin to Puckering, June 18 (ibid. i. 324) ; but Winwood, writing to Carleton, June 16, speaks of the Earl as still only dying (S. P. D., 1611_18, p. 237).

[6] Henry Howard, Earl of Northampton, brother of the Duke of Norfolk, attainted and beheaded in 1572, died unmarried. His great-nephew Thomas Howard, the Earl of Arundel, restored to the title in 1604, was the head of the Howard family. Chamberlain writes, ' He . . . left most of his land to the Earl of Arundel.' His house by Charing Cross he devised to his nephew the Earl of Suffolk for life, with remainder to Henry Howard, Suffolk's third son, together with 800l. a year on lands; but the bequest to Suffolk of his furniture and movables was revoked out of jealousy when dying, on hearing that Suffolk was to be appointed Treasurer. He dealt liberally with his followers, leaving most of them 100l. apiece. The three hospitals were (1) at Clun, in Shropshire ; (2) Castle

depraved manie wayes: he discontented those expected to be his
adopted heires, because he made them not equall with Arundell
his heire: yet he left them worth 40000^l & gave to his servants
& to 3 or more hospitalls &c. the 4ta parte of his estate in valewe:
by the liberall guifte of king James he had 3000^l per annum of
the Duke of Norfolk lands forfeted: & died therby & by his owne
acquisicion, being supposed under hand a frend to papistes, worth
about 120000^l: he was said to practise under hand the hinder-
ance of the subsidie demaunded, this parliament:[1] but it rather
semed his maiestie's deniall to remitt the late imposicions upon
merchandize imposed by the king's royall power 4 yeres past did
so dislike the commons that no subsidie was granted: & the new
elected & summoned parliament dissolved without any law passed:
& instantlie upon this strange event the Bishops, Lords of the
Councell & other his maiestie's best affected servaunts presented to
his maiestie voluntarie guiftes in money & plate:[2] but in no suche
measure, nor to be expected to draw on so manie givers (altho
the exemple be notified by letters of the Councell to all counties
in England) as is likelie to discharg a 4th part of his maiestie's
detts:[3] my owne gift was 50^l: grant o God that & thrice so
much may sett his maistie's estate in equall termes as it was at his
happie coronacion.

3 Masters of Wards died in 2 yeres.[4]

Rising, in Norfolk; (3) Greenwich. (See *Court and Times of James I.* vol. i.
pp. 324 and 325, where the letters of Chamberlain and Larkin are given in full;
and *Dict. Nat. Bio.*).

[1] The 'Addled Parliament,' which met on April 5, 1614, and was dissolved on
June 7. Northampton had opposed the summoning of a Parliament and was
believed to have induced a member, John Hoskins, to use insulting language
against the King's Scotch favourites, in the hope that the King would in displeasure
cause a dissolution (Gard. *Hist.* ii. 247–50).

[2] Before July 18, 1614, 23,000l. was thus collected. Some of the judges offered
under 20l., which was refused. The Earl of Salisbury gave the largest sum, 300l.
Suffolk, Somerset, and Coke gave 200l. (Chamberlain to Carleton, June 30, 1614;
Court and Times of James I. vol. i. p. 328.)

[3] The answer to the general appeal to the counties in two years only produced
42,600l. The total only came to 66,000l. In July 1614 the King's debts stood
at 700,000l., and there was an annual deficit of 61,000l. (Gard. *Hist.* ii. 260,
from a statement drawn up the day after Suffolk's accession to office.)

[4] (1) Robert Cecil, Earl of Salisbury, died May 24, 1612; (2) Sir George
Carew, died November 13, 1612; (3) Sir Walter Cope, died July 31, 1614.

October 1611 Lord Knolles [1] made M' of Wards, Sir Foulk Grevell Chauncellor of Exchequer,[2] Sir Julius Caesar [3] M' of Rolls :

Julie 1614. Erle of Suffolk made Lord Tresorer.[4]

In October after 1614 : [5] when the howse of Suffolk was at the highest pitchie : himself lord Tresorer, his son in law the erle of Somersett lord high chamberlain [6] & the most potent favorite in my tyme : lord Knollys another sonne in law Tresorer of the howsehold & by his favor made Master of Wards : [7] the erle of Salisbury another sonne in lawe : [8] the Lord Walden his eldest sonne maried the heire to the erle of Dumbarre,[9] another of the chief favorites to king James : all his yonger sonnes maried to liviugs of 1000ᶩ per annum & more : the chauncelor of exchequer & manie other great officers placed by his meanes & his sonne in lawe Somersett's, that grand favorite : having also built a howse or pallace called Awdeley End in Essex to the charges of 80 thowsand pounds at lest : & making councellors & bering chief sway at Councell Table & in Court & common welthe. Sodenlie I saie Somersett & his Countess in *October* 1614 were accused for poysoning Sir Thomas Overbery, prisoner in the Tower, being committed as was thought for a contempt in refusing an imployment as agent into

[1] October 10. Knollys had been appointed Treasurer of the Household in 1602. In 1614 he was one of the Commissioners of the Treasury.

[2] In succession to Sir Julius Cæsar.

[3] Sir Julius Cæsar, Wilbraham's colleague at the Court of Requests, and Chancellor of the Exchequer in 1606, had obtained a reversionary grant of the Mastership of the Rolls on Jan. 16, 1611 (Foss's *Judges*).

[4] July 10 (Gard. *Hist.* ii. 259).   [5] *I.e.* October 1615.

[6] Married Frances Howard, the divorced Countess of Essex, daughter of the Earl of Suffolk, Dec. 26, 1613 ; appointed Lord Chamberlain in succession to Suffolk, July 1614.

[7] Master of the Wards Oct. 10, 1614 ; married Suffolk's third daughter ; Lord Treasurer of the Household, 1602.

[8] William, second Earl of Salisbury, married Lady Catherine Howard, Suffolk's youngest daughter.

[9] Theophilus Howard, created Lord Howard of Walden 1610 ; married in 1612 Lady Elizabeth Home, daughter of George Home, Earl of Dunbar (*Dict. Nat. Bio.*).

[10] Sir Fulke Greville, appointed Chancellor of the Exchequer October 161 remaining in office till 1621.

some remote country :[1] but beleved to be committed by a practise because he being late before Somersett's bedfellow, mynion & inward councellor, for which he was much envyed in Courte, he was enemy to that mariage of Somersett with the countesse his wief late before divorced by a most solemne & straung sentence,[2] because Essex was *quoad illam maleficiatus* : for this poisoning the lieutenant of the Tower[3] & 3 more[4] suffred in Michaelmas terme 1615 : & this 16 of *May* Somersett & his ladie expected to be tryed by Peers : but difference upon unknowen cause : & this business hath entertayned England &c. with talke.

In Whitson Week[5] 1616 the Erle of Somersett & his Countesse were severallie arrayned before Peeres : she confessed the fact : he denyed & answared to the proefes : & both condemned.

In *May* 1616 : the king gave up the protection & keping of the Cawtionari Townes in Holland &c : & they have & are to pay 200000l[6] which they owed to Quene Elizabeth : which wilbe a supplie to the king's cofers for a short tyme : by this some think we loose honor & our footing in that strong neheburhod : others think they will depend of our protection still :

In the end of *June* 1616 : Coke, lord chief justice,[7] was convented before the King & his councell at divers tymes, &

---

[1] The King had proposed to Overbury a diplomatic appointment. On his refusal Overbury was committed to the Tower on April 21, 1613. His death took place there on September 15. It was not until July 1615 that information came to Winwood which speedily led to the implication of the Earl and Countess in his murder.

[2] The judgment of divorce was pronounced on Sept. 25, 1613, two months before the marriage of the Countess to Somerset.

[3] Sir Gervase Helwys.

[4] Weston, Mrs. Turner, and the apothecary Franklin.

[5] The Countess was tried on May 24, 1616 ; the Earl on May 25.

[6] In MS. 2,000,000l., but this must be an error for 200,000l. The agreement was for 215,000l. in all, of which sum 15,000l. was to go to the officers of the garrisons and 200,000l. to the Exchequer. The debt of the provinces to England was to be cancelled (Gard. *Hist.* ii. 383).

[7] Chief Justice of the King's Bench since Oct. 25, 1613. On June 30, 1616, Coke was sequestered from the Council Table and ordered to 'forbear to ride the summer circuit.'

sequestred from his chief justice & councellor's place : that had ben most in wind & forward in prosecuting Somersett &c. for poysoning Overberie : [1] he is for welth & law witt above all of memorie : if he spend it will not unlike to be restored : [2] he is taxed to have practised a *praemunire* against the Lord chancellor : [3] a litle before his fall, Sir Fr. Bacon, attorney generall, was sworne councellor.[4] His arrogancie lost him many freinds, to help him in neede.

Julie 1616 : Sir John Roper [5] Hollis [6] } lorded at 10000[1] price a peece as is thought to supplie the progresse of the lord Hay in his magnificent ambassage to Fraunce.

[Henceforward the MS. continues in another hand.]

Jan. 4, 1641 : [7] the King came to the house of commons with an armed trayn to seise upon the 5 members.

Decemb. 6, 7, the army seised & stopped many members & deterred others ; seised 45, imprisoning them ; secluded 98 besides others that withdrew.[8]

[1] He was one of the commissioners nominated to examine into the Overbury murder, and presided at the several trials arising therefrom.

[2] Coke was finally discharged from his office in November 1616, after Wilbraham's death ; in Sept. 1617 he was restored to the Council Table, and in 1618 he was appointed one of the Commissioners of the Treasury, but his return to favour was short-lived.

[3] In the c ses of Glanville and Allen, two swindlers against whom recourse had been had to the equitable jurisdiction of Chancery from the strict rules of the Common Law Courts ; Coke, by a forced construction of 27 Edward III., St. 1, cap. i., enacting the penalty attached to a præmunire against those who appealed to Rome from sentences obtained in the King's Courts, instigated these two swindlers to prefer an indictment in the King's Bench not only against the suitors who had obtained the protection of Chancery, but also against the counsellors and clerks who had shared in the proceedings (Gard. *Hist.* iii. 10–13).

Attorney-General Oct. 27, 1613 ; Privy Councillor June 9, 1616.

[5] Lord Teynham.   [6] Lord Houghton.   [7] 1642.

[8] This must refer to Pride's Purge, December 6, 1648. Dr. Gardiner puts the number of members placed under restraint on Dec. 6 at forty-one (*Hist. of the Civil War*, iv. 270) ; but two, Rudyard and Fiennes, being soon liberated, and a few, like Major-General Browne, arrested some days later, the total number of members in confinement was forty-five, as here ; whilst ninety-six others were turned back (*ibid.* p. 273).

1645, EXPRESSIONS OF MR. ARTHUR WODENOTH.[1]

They that are not touched with a sense of the present distrae-
tions, and divisions of Church and State are either somwhat more
or some thing less then men.

I know some there be, that conceave the distance already so
great as cannot be composed : and others that expect noe good
untill things be brought to a greater extremity.   These are
buckets, tho hanging at the same pole, the depression of the one
is the exaltation of the other.   What shall wee now doe, embark
our selves in a party, and launch out into the sea of dissention
which casts up nothing but myre and dyrt, to the preiudice and
contempt of all propositions for accomodations, God forbid, for
although it be true, that some are soe necessarily involved in these
differences as a deserting of them were a betraying if not the truth,
at least the trust, reposed in them, yet is it as true, that wee whoe
are plac'd in a lower forme may nether propose nor prosecute any
thing beyond that orbe and sphere wherein God hath placed us.—
Uzzah's good intention proved too weak a helmett to ward of God's
stroke for his profanitie.[2]   Not to mention the differences in the
State which are too much encreased by the mentioning, in the
Church the great stirr (and its very great) is not soe much about
the body or more essentiall part of religion as about the cloathes or
ornament wherewith it is presented.   Wee are agreed that there

---

[1] The friend of George Herbert.   Isaac Walton, in his account of the rebuilding
by Herbert of the ruined church of Layton Ecclesia, speaks of the bounty of Mr.
Nicholas Ferrar (of Little Gidding) and 'Mr. Arthur Woodnot,' describing
Wodenoth as a goldsmith in Foster Lane, London, who, 'having obtained so much
as to be able to show some mercy to the poor and preserve a competence for himself, dedicated the remaining part of his life to the service of God, and to be useful
for his friends ; and he proved to be so to Mr. Herbert' (*Walton's Lives*, 3rd ed.
vol. ii. pp. 57, 58).   Three weeks before George Herbert's death 'his old and dear
friend Mr. Woodnot came from London to Bemerton and never left him till he had
seen him draw his last breath and closed his eyes on his death-bed.'   Herbert
appointed him his sole executor (*ibid.* pp. 120, 124). Apparently he may be identified
with Arthur Wodenoth, twelfth son of John Wodenoth, of Shavinton, Cheshire.
His aunt Mary was the mother of Nicholas Ferrar of Little Gidding, whose cousin
he therefore was (Ormerod's *Cheshire*, iii. 508, pedigree of Woodnoths of Shavinton).

[2] 2 Samuel vi. 3–7.

is noe power whence wee can derive or deduce the forme of God's worship, but from God himself, that the holy Scripture contayne the revealed will of God and are able to make us wise to salvation. That prayer, preaching, and the Sacrament are God's owne ordinances whereby hee conveighs grace and mercy to the soules of his servants : but whether in prayer wee should be tyed to a forme or left at lyberty, whoe should preach and by what authority, whether the Cross or gesture of kneeling should be us'd or omitted in the Sacraments, these and the lyke are the things that occasion our quarrell. And truly might I without offence speak my thoughts, I should say that the differences in these things are not soe essentially materiall but might admitt of a charitable construction from the opposers. St. Paul's lyberty and moderation, in observing or not observing a day, eating or not eating, may be admitted in these cases for imitation. Therefore lett not him that prayeth by a forme iudge him that prays without, nor hee that admitts of the cross or makes scruple of kneeling, condemn the contrary, but rather receave one another as Christ alsoe received us to the glory of God, for certainly as the influences of spirituall lyfe are not soe much from participation with all other members, as from communion with the Lord Jesus Christ the head, soe neither doe these outward ceremonies, ether in the observation, (soe it be free from superstition) nor in the omission, (soe it be cleare from contempt) ether preiudice or promote true piety in any proportion to the more materiall parts of religion ; so that it is iustly to be wondered at and seriously lamented, that Protestants who of all people under heaven have the most perfect example and exact rule of charity to walk by, should yet be so uncharitable each to other, and that in the prosecution of the wayes of piety, which if true are all sodered and cimented by love ; I shall not presume to assigne any other grounds of these dissentions besides Sathan's malice and the pride of our owne corrupt natures, whereunto may be added the iust difference betweene a regenerate and an unregenerate estate, or they may arise from less materiall considerations as the meanes whereby or the manner how God works regeneration, the severall degrees or measures of sanctification, besides the different constitu tions of naturall temper which shew themselves in our spirituall performancy. The cure of these differences certainly would be exceedingly promoted, by an observation of that catholike rule required by our Lord and Master as the condition of admittance into his services, which is a denyall of our selves and taking up our cross.   These would rightly dispose us to follow him in that other lesson of meekness and humility, and these togeather would ether take away, or much abate our private dissentions.

Heare I shall crave leave to the praise of the glory of God's grace in his beloved, to mention what God in mercy did for my soule by the operation of his holy spirit with his ordinances as theis are administered in the congregation of Protestants in the Church of England :

Wherein I shall declare
- Antecedents more { Remote / Neare
- Concomitants both { outward means / inward effects
- Consequents by theire { nature / continuance.

In all God's free Grace to a wretched sinner.

In the first I might look so fare back as to childhood, but as hereof I observed little, so would it be to little purpose to say much : about the age of 14 years I was sent to London to be an aprentise, more ignorant of the ways of God then was credible, in excuse of which, I can say noe more, then that there was noe preaching Minister all that tyme in the place where I had my birth and breeding : shortly after I came to London, where by the noxious course of some friends my intended imployment was deserted and I left to more vacancy, then was convenient to a youth at his entrance : upon what ground, or whose incitation I now remember not I was inclined to goe to Lectures, which I usually did twice a week, and hereby receaved both information of judgment and better composure of affections then before.   After the expence of 2 yeares I was put to a Master where I mett with very little concurrance of naturall affections, though with some sutableness to my apprehentions, and thus much of the *more remote antecedents*. Of the *more neare*, the first occation was the drawing on of Easter, when both custome and iniunction prompt to the Communion, in consideration whereof my thoughts minded mee of a dangerous fitt of sickness which had befallen mee the yeare before, and seemd to poynt my apprehension of the unworthy receaving of the Sacrament (notwithstanding I had beene catechised by the Minister) as the cause which moulded my mynd into a more serious consultation how to obtaine the benefitt, and avoyd the danger: for which purpose by such meanes as were concurrant with my condition I endevord preparation, and in want of liberty to heare sermons, and oportunity of discourse with men, was glad to apply my self to bookes: when came to my hands one of Parsons published by Bunny,[1] in reading whereof I mett with a relation of St. Austine's conversion, whereupon my thoughts began to mutiny and by way of sillogism thus to dispute. Austin that was thus miraculously converted was a saynt of God: the premises being acknowledged both by Papist and Protestants, the conclusion would necessarily follow, that, that Religion of which St. Austine was, is the true Christian Religion, but whether the Papist or Protestant doe more truely lay clayme to St. Austin and hould that Religion whereof hee was, I could find noe way to satisfy myself. By this I became sensible as well of the neglect of others, as my owne defects in not being better grounded in the principles of Christian Religion, whereby I was equally unable to encounter the assaultes, which were scandell to others if I refused to come to the Communion, and sinn against conscience if I came doubtingly, from both which Sathan. suggested a remedy worse then the dissease, which was the renouncing of my religion. I shall not need to tell them that have had trouble in their consciences what I suffred, and if I should declare it unto others they would not regard it. The time thrusting mee on to a resolution, I bethought my self of our Minister, and from those reciprocall expressions which the Scripture makes of Pastor and People, I resolved to address my self unto him: for the avoyding mistakes, either in my expressions or his apprehentions, I digested my doubts into writing: having obtained leave in my way I mett with a kinsman of my owne then fellow of a colledg;[2]

[1] *A Book of Christian Exercise appertaining to Resolution, perused and accompanied now with a Treatise tending to Pacification*, 1584, 8vo, and repeatedly republished. The first part is a portion of a treatise by the Jesuit Robert Parsons, with certain alterations by Edmund Bunny, who united the part of a pluralist in prebendal stalls with that of an itinerant Calvinistic preacher. Parsons had given to this work only his initials, R. P., and Bunny appropriated it without knowing who was the author. By this book Richard Baxter at fourteen was first turned to serious thoughts (*Dict. Nat. Bio.*).

[2] Probably his cousin, Nicholas Ferrar, of Little Gidding, 'at an early age made Fellow of Clare Hall, in Cambridge, where he continued to be eminent for his piety, temperance, and learning' (Walton's *Lives*, ii. 106). For the relationship

and as they that are touched ether with payne of body or affliction
of mynd are not nyce in discovering theire infirmities I shewed
him of my troubles: hee was pleased to manifest a great measure
both of affection and wisdome, in accommodating proper and particular remedies to my severall scruples: in the close, for better
security he refer'd mee to a booke of Dr. John White entitled,
the way to the true Church,[1] wherein I found a discussion and
resolution of those which Sathan's malice and my own ignorance
had generated: by God's blessing upon these meanes I attayned
to calmness of mind with desire after the holy Communion.   And
thus much of the *Antecedents*: the *concommitants*, the *outward
meanes* were prayer, receaving the Sacrament, and hearing the
Word preached, which I mention in this order because in this order
I was made partaker of them that day: in respect of the rehearsall
sermon[2] at Paul's cross, in the morning there was none at our
Church, but after service the Communion celebrated, which I
receaved both with affection and comfort; in the afternoone I went
unto an other church wher I heard a sermon upon the first and
second verses of the 3rd chapter, to the Coloss. : if *yee be risen with
Christ seek those things which are above, where Christ sitteth on the
right hand of God: sett your affections on things above, and not on
things on the earth*.   And now I am come to the *inward effect*, which
if I could represent to your apprehensions I should not need to
bespeak your attentions.   The highest pinacle of Solomon's glory
did noe more transcend the lowest depth of Job's misery, then the
ioy I now had, did the greatest comfort which before I ever felt.
The Counterpane of that decree of Election which was made by the
eternall Councell of God before tyme in heaven, was at this tyme,
signed, seald and delivered by his holy Spirrit accompanying his
ordinances in the congregation of his servants on earth.   And now

see Ormerod's *Cheshire*, iii. 508.   Nicholas Ferrar and Arthur Wodenoth were the
chief friends of George Herbert, and are several times mentioned together by
Walton.

[1] *The Way to the True Church ; wherein the principal Motives perswading to
Romanisme are familiarly disputed and driven to their Issues.*   London, 1608, 4to.
Dr. John White was born in 1570 ; admitted as a sizar to Caius College, Cambridge, 1586 (B.A. 1589_90, M.A. 1593, D.D. 1612) ; Vicar of Eccles 1606, Rector
of Barsham 1609, and in 1614 or 1615 appointed Chaplain in Ordinary to James I.
died 1615. (*Dict. Nat. Bio.*).

[2] See *ante*, p. 13, note 3.

tell mee if you can, what this ioy is, but as they that have not felt it cannot imagine it, so neither can they that have, fully express it.

At last I am arrived at the *consequence* or effects which flowed from this fountaine and rann in three streames.

1 fayth in God : 2^d righteousness toward man : 3^{tly} contentation with my present condition. Fayth is that grace of God which ingrafts us into Christ Jesus our Lord, and is made evident by the effects and fruites, 1 a full assurance of the pardon and forgiveness of my sinns, & that God reconcil'd mee to himself, and 2^{ndly} noe less evidence that I should never fall totally away from him, but by his mercy be preserved unto eternall life and salvation : another, because of the same streame, was a breathing after and delight in God's ordinances, in prayer, as the breathings of the soule after heaven, in preaching as the food of spirituall life, in the sacraments as a visible representation of Christ's death and passion, and an undoubted confirmation of the benefitts thereof. A third was an enlargment of soule in the prayses of God with love to the society of his servants, and desire that others might partake of that grace and mercy which God had shewed unto mee. 2nd Righteousness towards man was declared both in deeds and words : in deeds, 1° by a sincere and faythfull performance of the duty of a servant, in which relation I then stood : there was now noe eye of my master necessary to quicken my obedience or to regulate my practice, which were carried on with that assiduity as might seeme to render my master alwayes present. In words, for the truth whereof I refused not to expose myself to the greatest hazard : those commands of my Master and Mistris which hitherto had carryed all before them, had now noe force, more then what was consonant to God's commands, which had an influence upon all my performances, and therefore receaving a commaund to deny a truth I chose rather to deny that commaund and render myself obnoxious to the severest punishment of my Master (and it sometimes was severe) then to disobey the least commaund of my God : the same apprehention which required observance, in what was right forbad obedience, in that was contrary. 3rd was contentation with my present condicion which however in it self most mean and contemptible, and such as seem'd inconsistant with the least contentment, yet by god's mercy was advantagious to my present comfort. None ever gathered greater accommodations from the concurrance of all

earthly delights, then I now did from my low condition, whereby
the variation of my course was made more easy, and those interrup-
tions which prosperity casts in the way to heaven removed : another
effect was sobriety, which commanded both my will and affections
and at once cutt off those luxurious branches, which had sprung
either from conformity with the world or carnall satisfactions :
those favours or fancyes which till now I either enioyed with delight
or desyred as pretious reliques, had a bill of divorce put into theire
hands never to be readmitted, being not to be retayned without an
abatement of spirituall comfort.   And thus much of the *consequence*,
for their nature ; theire continuance is the last.   Herein, as in all,
God's free grace was the hinge whereupon all depended and whilst
turnd towards him, yeilded nothing but soule ravishing delight
and contentment, in manifesting to my owne conscience the truth
of my conversion against all doubts and suspition.   But least these
might either coole or occation too much security, the hinge, though
hang'd upon the unalterable decree of God's free grace in Christ
Jesus, yet seemed to turn backwards and I left rather by consideration to understand then by sence to feele the sweetness of these
comforts : thus at sometimes were the former ioyes interrupted.
From this true though otherwise imperfect narration, these conclu-
sions I conceave will result : first that true conversion is a sincere
desire and endeavour after an universall reformation and performance of our particular places, accompanied with a deniall of all
ungodliness and worldly lusts, and with that unseparable trinity
of Christian graces, holyness, righteousness and sobriety, soe farr
forth as may be attayned during this lyfe, wherein these graces are
imperfect : 2*ly*, that where this conversion is ordinarily wrought,
there the holy spirritt of God doth beare wittnes to the truth for
substance though not warrant the perfection for forme of his outward worship and service : 3dly that men in the present forme of
administration of divine ordinances, in the congregation of Protestants, in the Church of England, the holy spirrit of God doth
concurr ordinarily to the worke of true conversion, and also by the
same administration, worketh repentance for such breaches and
incursions as sinn dayly makes upon the soules of God's servants.
The premises considered, my humble petition to them that have
found these effects in theire soules is that they would not draw
back, nor forsake those assemblies where by theire owne experience
they have found that God in mercy doth so carry on and preser[ve]

the power of his owne ordinances as neither humane constitutions, mixt congregations or personall sinns, can interrupt those ends whereunto hee hath appointed them. And to them that have not yet found these effects, my petition lykewise is, that avoyding preiudice against the form of administration of the ordinances, or the persons, or places, they will in humility and patience wayte upon God in that way wherein they have his promise that they shall, and the testimony of his servants that they have found pardon and peace thorough Jesus Christ our Lord, to whom be glory for evermore.

POSTSCRIPT, I would not have added more but to remove a double charge which is layd against mee by freinds of contrary apprehensions : some will have mee to be a superstitious formalist and others enclinable to the separatists : whereunto I answare, true and not true. In theire apprehensions possibly true, in the things themselves not true : if by superstitious formalist; they understand one that frequents the Church and congregation where God's ordinances are administered and desireth all things there should be done with reverence, decency and order, that thither nether brings, nor there willingly exerciseth any carnal affection, that puts an equall esteeme upon all God's ordinances, that shews reverence to ministers (notwithstanding some personall infirmities) for theire works' sake, and in some cases makes addresses to them, for solution of doubts, though not for absolution of sinns, that unto tymes, places and things sett a part for divine service hath such respect as is meet without superstition, that approves such abstinence in dyett, apparell, and other carnall contentments as may weaken naturall corruptions with least observance, I confess I am a superstitious formalist. But and if by formalist they understand one that puts religion in observation of humane constitutions, bowing to or towards the communion table and worshipping towards the East, that doth bodily reverence without inward devotion or apprehension of his Maiesty at that most sweet and most pretious name of my Lord and Master Jesus, that accompts ecclesiastical cannons equall to the cannon of holy scripture, that esteemes very highly of service anthems, homilies, and church catechisme, with the neglect of the minister, prayer, preaching, singing of psalmes and all other instructions, I am no formalist.

So and if by separatist they understand one that makes scruple

of doing any thing in God's service but what is warranted by his
word, that desireth the whole congregation of the Lord were holy,
that prophane and scandalous livers might be sharply reproved
and, if incorrigible, excommunicated untill they had repented, that
all reliques of popery and superstitious pictures were utterly
abolished, that in all companies wee endeavour to promote God's
glory, and to edify one another, I am a separatist.

But if by separatist they understand such as refuse all forms ot
God's service and ether omitts comming to the congregation or
there by unreverent behaviour manifests his contempt of the
service, that shuns all assemblies but those of his owne iudgment,
and all Ministers but such as themselves have elected which are
not alwayes so very well qualified, that will not baptise children
because not expressed in the Scripture to their apprehen(sion),
that accompts all humane learning and arts unnecessary for inter-
preting the holy Scripture, that hath a preiudice against the use
of the Lord's prayer and singing psalms, I am no separatist.

Nor ever yett concurr'd soe farr in theire opinions or practice as
to be present at any meeting or private fast that lookes that way.
Whether Episcopacy, Presbetery or Independency be most sutable
to the holy scripture, or that therein there is such a particular and
exact forme of discipline prescribed as doth necessarily commaund
observance upon paine of God's displeasure, I confess I doe not
understand. Nor will I presume to iudg the expediency or un-
expediency of an enforced liturgie, nor vex myself with feares least
that now in force might suffer some change or variation, which
possibly the constitutions of person, and tymes may have made
convenient: I may not iustify those that altogether omitt the
Lord's prayer nor commend them that use all other as a preface to
it: I equally blame them that refuse to come to sermons either
because there be prayers or because there be noe prayers: I will
soe farr shunn Armenianism, as not to attribute the least inclination toward goodness to the utmost endeavour of nature: And I
will also beware of such sloathfullness as may retard Christian
duty or betray me to that horrid apprehension, which that I may
be the less guilty would charge the sinn upon God's most holy
decree. I will neither so undervalew humane learning as to
deprive it of its due honour nor soe doate upon it as to conceave it
should unlock those cabinetts of God's secretts which he reveales
onely to them that feare him: I dare not subscribe to ether

opinion. Sunday a Sabboth or Sunday noe Saboth, the one may be too rigyd, the other too remiss: I am neither against King nor Parliament but for both, peaceably submitting to what the Lawes of God rightly understood and the good laws of the land rightly declared impose upon mee, if extream necessity enforce.

I shall rather suffer as a patient that I doe not, then doe as an agent what I know not. I will not chase iustice with more speed then they can safely drive that have the flocks before them, least my precipitancy preiudice them that are bigg with sorrow, and soe theire repentence become abortive: better many delinquants were delay'd then that one true penitent should be preiudiced. These are matters too high and wonderfull for mee, I cannot attain unto them, and possibly it is not my unhappiness to be thus bounded, for who hath been either a bringer up, or a voluntiere in these divisions and is guilty of less error then the not observing each word of commaund; as noe popular applause shall prompt mee on to any unwarrantable action, so neither shall any opprobrious name of Puritaine, Roundhead, etc. (by God's grace) deterre mee from performance of any Christian duty; of my own choice 1 will not break the rank wherein God hath placed mee, nor by his grace refuse to doe or suffer what hee shall appoynt unto mee, until further manifestation, whereof I shall make my humble supplication that hee, which took away the wall of separation from betweene Jew and Gentile, and that he might reconcile man unto God, took our nature into the unity of his owne person, will of his infinite mercy create peace between them who profess the maintenance of his true religion to be the cause of their divisions, that noe more of their blood be shedd, for redemption of whom Christ shedd his most precious blood, or if hee have appointed the sword in the hand of the souldier rather then his word in the mouth of his minister to be the way whereby hee will pacify his Church and establish his Gospell, that hee will make it knowne unto his servant who hopes hee desires to feare his name, and yett is not soe satisfyed that he can either assent to those doctrines that encourage to warr, though delivered from the pulpitt in his name, nor say amen to those prayers which in the same place are against peace, though put up to his Maiestie, but must Wayte the further manifestation of his will, and in the meane space, with Elihu in Job [1]

---

[1] Job xxxiv. 32.

pray, *Lord what I see not teach thou me, And if I have done iniquity I will doe soe no more. finis.*

1648 *Jan.* 19.   King Charles was brought by a part of the army from Wyndsor to St. James, next day to Westminster to Sir Robert Cotton's house : the King's bench & chancery being ioyned in one and scaffolded, the Lord President Serieant Bradshaw with his trayn carryed up, the mace born by Serieant Dendy,[1] the sword by Coll. Humfreys, before him, and after him about 70 Commissioners,[2] Mʳ Asky[3] a lawyer of the Temple, Dr. Dorislaus[4] a cyvilian, Mʳ Cook[5] a lawyer of Gray's Inn Sollicitor Generall for the business. The commission by which the Court satt being read, Commissioners called, the Lord President commaunded the seriant at armes to fetch the prysoner, who brought the Kyng and placed him in a chayre : the Lord President said they were there assembled by authority of the Commons of England to try Charles Stewart, King of England, who had betrayed the trust reposed in him by the Commons of England, and commaunded his charge to

[1] Edward Dendy, Sergeant at Arms.

[2] Sixty-eight answered to their names (Gardiner's *Civil War*, iv. 299).

[3] Richard Aske or Asky, admitted Inner Temple 1606, called to the Bar January 29, 1615 (*Cal. of the Inner Temple Records*, ii. 88) ; Bencher 1633 (*ibid.* p. 211) ; counsel for Strode, 1629 ; appointed by the Houses Coroner and Attorney of the King's Bench, 1644 ; Junior Counsel at the King's trial, Sergeant and Justice of the Upper Bench, June 1, 1649 ; died 1656 (Foss's *Judges*).

[4] Dr. Isaac Dorislaus, by birth Dutch, Judge Advocate to Essex in 1642 : Judge of the Court of Admiralty, 1648 ; assisted in the preparation of the charge against the King ; sent by the Commonwealth to the Hague, where he was assassinated by a party of Cavaliers in May 1649 (*Dic. Nat. Bio.*).

[5] John Cook, or Cooke, son of Isaac Cook, of Burbridge, co. Leicester, Esquire, admitted to Gray's Inn Nov. 1, 1623 (Foster's *Gray's Inn Register of Admissions*, p. 171) ; called to the Bar Nov. 21, 1631 (*Gray's Inn Pension Book*, p. 309) ; called to be of the *Grand Company* May 24, 1650 (*ibid.* p. 376). There is a long letter of his to Strafford when Lord Lieutenant in Ireland, printed in *Camden Miscellany*, vol. ix., *Strafford Papers*, p. 14, where Cook is said to have been employed in revising an edition of the Statutes (*Mercurius Elencticus*, No. 56, 1649, cited there). After acting as Solicitor-General in the trial of the King and that of Hamilton, and his fellow officers, he was, in December 1647, appointed Chief Justice of Munster, and in 1655 Justice of the Court of Upper Bench in Ireland. On October 16, 1660, he was executed as a regicide. At a Pension held July 4, 1660, it had been ordered that his chambers should be seized (*Gray's Inn Pension Book,* p. 431).

be read, which done, the King would have spoke, but the Sollicitor Generall sayd : ' I doe in the name of the Commons of England charg Charles Stewart, King of England, with Tyranny, murther and treason : ' cheif heads were for levying warr & calling in the Irish. The King demaunds to know their authority, which hee owned not.

The week following they goe to prove the charge, which done, his sentence was read upon Saturday, *Jan.* 27, 1648 : and Tuesday about two of the clock it was put in execution by taking off the King's head att his Court gate. Hee was third sonn of King James, born in Scotland Nov. 19, 1600, was created Duke of York at White hall Jan. 6, 1604, and Nov. 4, 1616, hee was created Prince of Wales & Earl of Chester, began his raign March 27, 1625, raigned near 24 yeares : professed himself a Protestant att his death, forgave his executioner and all others whose hands were in that his unnaturall death.

Feb. 9, Duke Hamleton,[1] Erl of Norwitch, Lord Capell [2] and Sir John Owen [3] were one by one brought to the same barr, the same Lord President sitting with other Commissioners,[4] but the same Sollicitor Generall impeaching them. Duke pleaded the command of the Parliament of Scotland, Capell, quarter as a souldier,[5] Owen not guilty.

[1] James, Duke of Hamilton, commander of the Scotch army in the second Civil War, capitulated with the remnant of his force at Uttoxeter, Aug. 25, 1648, having ' the lives and safety of their persons assured to them ' (Gard. *Civil War*, iv. 192).

[2] George Goring, Earl of Norwich, and Arthur Lord Capel surrendered at Colchester, Aug. 27, 1648. The superior officers submitted to mercy, but Norwich and Capel had received, the day after the signing of the capitulation, an assurance from Fairfax of quarter for their lives (*ibid.* iv. 201–6).

[3] Sir John Owen headed a rising in North Wales in June 1648.

[4] On Feb. 3, 1649, Parliament erected a new High Court of Justice to try these prisoners. Dr. Gardiner gives the date of the opening of proceedings as Feb. 10 (*History of the Commonwealth*, i. 11–12).

[5] These pleas were not admitted, as Hamilton was born after the accession of James I., and so came within the *Post nati* judgment, and in Capel's case a military promise was held as not binding on a civil court.

INDEX